Advance Prai[...]

Above All, Be Kind

D[...] you want to raise children who know who they are and what is truly important in life? If you do, this book will be tremendously helpful. Practical and profound, full of real life examples, *Above All Be Kind* is a wonderful guide to helping your children to be joyful, self-confident, and caring people.

— John Robbins, author of *Diet For A New America*, founder of EarthSave International, and father of Ocean Robbins

Profound, practical, positive and potentially pivotal, this book is a vital tool in the struggle to raise healthy and happy children who know the joy and richness of service and compassion. Recommended reading for parents, teachers, aunts, uncles — everyone who loves children and wants to see them thrive.

— Ocean Robbins, Founder, Youth for Environmental Sanity (YES!), co-author, *Choices for Our Future,* and father of twin boys

Above All Be Kind is a lovely book, written in a personal idiom distinguished by insight, common sense, intelligence and love. When I finished reading it I wanted to hug Zoe Weil. You will too.

— John Taylor Gatto, author, *The Underground History of American Education* and *D[...]ng Us Down*

As a parent of six children I found *Above All Be Kind* the greatest advice I have ever read about raising children. Zoe Weil's book will not only make you a better parent, it will make you a better human being.

— Howard F. Lyman LL.D, author of *Mad Cowboy* and President, Voice for a Viable Future

Above All, Be Kind is one of the most important books in the humane education movement. It is written with clarity, conviction, courage, and hope. Hard facts along with deep compassion and heart fill its pages. This book will empower children and adults to act to make this a more peaceful, sustainable, and humane world. No matter how much your day is filled with busy-ness, above all, read this book and share its brilliance.

— Marc Bekoff, author of *Minding Animals*, co-author (with Jane Goodall) of *The Ten Trusts: What We Must Do To Care For The Animals We Love* and cofounder of Ethologists for the Ethical Treatment of Animals

Above All, Be Kind

Raising a Humane Child in Challenging Times

ZOE WEIL

NEW SOCIETY PUBLISHERS

Cataloguing in Publication Data:

A catalog record for this publication is available from the National Library of Canada.

Cover design by John Nedwidek (emdesign). Cover image © Corbis.

Printed in Canada by Transcontinental.
Third Printing, December, 2004.

Paperback ISBN: 0-86571-493-2

Inquiries regarding requests to reprint all or part of *Above All, Be Kind* should be addressed to New Society Publishers at the address below.

To order directly from the publishers, please add $4.50 shipping to the price of the first copy, and $1.00 for each additional copy (plus GST in Canada). Send check or money order to:

New Society Publishers
P.O. Box 189, Gabriola Island, BC V0R 1X0, Canada
1-800-567-6772

New Society Publishers' mission is to publish books that contribute in fundamental ways to building an ecologically sustainable and just society, and to do so with the least possible impact on the environment, in a manner that models this vision. We are committed to doing this not just through education, but through action. We are acting on our commitment to the world's remaining ancient forests by phasing out our paper supply from ancient forests worldwide. This book is one step towards ending global deforestation and climate change. It is printed on acid-free paper that is **100% old growth forest-free** (100% post-consumer recycled), processed chlorine free, and printed with vegetable based, low VOC inks. For further information, or to browse our full list of books and purchase securely, visit our website at: www.newsociety.com

NEW SOCIETY PUBLISHERS   www.newsociety.com

NOTE:

The names and some of the details in the stories have been changed to protect the privacy and identities of individual people.

CONTENTS

To Forest,
my beloved son,
and to Edwin,
my partner on the journey.

If we are to reach real peace in this world and if we are to carry on a real war against war, we shall have to begin with children; and if they will grow up in their natural innocence, we won't have to struggle, we won't have to pass fruitless idle resolutions, but we shall go from love to love and peace to peace, until at last all the corners of the world are covered with that peace and love for which consciously or unconsciously the whole world is hungering.

— MAHATMA GANDHI

INTRODUCTION

*Do something today which the
world may talk of hereafter.*

— Admiral Collingswood

THE GATHERING OF MOTHERS

A group of mothers was gathered for their monthly potluck dinner. One of the women had just gotten back from a trip out of state to visit an old high school friend, and she told the group that her seven-year-old spent the weekend playing Nintendo with her friend's older boys: "I tried to get him to come to the kitchen for lunch, but he was completely unresponsive and glued to the screen. Even though I was only a few feet away, I had to raise my voice to get his attention. He wouldn't even look away from the TV to ask me to bring him a bag of chips!" Although it had been a beautiful fall weekend, none of the boys played outside. Then she said, "On the drive home, he was so rude and disrespectful. I felt like I was coming back with a different boy."

Another mom quickly piped in to share a story about her nine-year-old son: "Tyler got home after playing at a friend's house last week, and he told me about pictures on the computer of naked people doing 'gross stuff' together. He asked if we could look for the pictures on our computer. It turns out an older neighborhood boy found a pornographic site on the Internet and told Tyler and his friend about it, in great detail."

At that point, the mother of a thirteen-year-old girl confessed, "My daughter has started wearing really skimpy, seductive clothes. We've been having awful fights about it. She says all her friends dress like that, and I'm just a prude. She seems to have utter disdain for me these days, and I've got no idea how to reach her."

Another added, "I'm glad I don't have these problems with my five-year-old, but I *am* worried about her. She won't eat anything but macaroni and cheese and French fries. She sits in front of the TV for hours, and she's really putting on weight. I'm scared to say anything, though. The last thing I want is for her to grow up with an eating disorder."

Then another woman spoke about her six-year-old son's recent experience at a birthday party: "Luke came home with a party favor bag filled with twenty-eight things. I counted them! They were all plastic junk, and everything was broken and in the trash by the end of the week. I was really disgusted by the waste, but Luke was so sad about all the broken toys that he wanted to go out and get *more*."

There was a long pause. Finally one mother asked: "Well, what do we *really* want most for our children?" One by one, each woman was able to share a fervent hope for her child. The mother of the Nintendo-loving boy said, "I want my son to be able to find joy and pleasure in imaginative play, rather than television and video games." Another mother said, "I want Julia to have good self-esteem and not be so susceptible to every trend." The mother whose son came home with the party favors declared, "I want Luke to value what is really important in life and not become materialistic." Another said, "I want my son to be honest so that I can trust him." The mother of the teenage daughter had tears in her eyes when she told the group, "I want Sarah to have compassion and respect for others and not be so irresponsible and insolent." Then she added, "I want her to have self-respect, too."

THE PROMISE OF RAISING A HUMANE CHILD

There is a word that sums up the qualities these mothers want most for their children. That word is *humane*. *Humane* literally means "having what are considered the best qualities of human beings." The humane child is not materialistic, cynical or snide, and the latest fad does not threaten to eclipse her deepest values. She sparkles with warmth and curiosity. She is gentle, yet also courageous and disciplined. Her spirit is vital, and her heart is full of love.

There are ways to raise your children to embody these qualities. If you embark on the journey to raise your children to be humane, they will know who they are and what is truly important in life. They will meet the world with integrity. Humane children are nourished by deeply held values that help them resist peer pressure and cultural messages that are shallow or dangerous. They believe in themselves and their ability to make a positive contribution with their lives. Such children are successful in the deepest meaning of the word because they are empowered to follow their dreams without harming others in the process.

As their parent, you too will find greater meaning and depth in your life when you set out to raise your children to be humane. Together with your children you will be able to explore the joys and satisfactions that life can bring when lived with the most abiding humane values. Instead of being alienated from one another, you and your children will forge ever deepening connections marked by understanding and mutual respect.

In this book you will learn how to raise your children to be humane within their families and communities. But you will also discover tools to raise your children to be humane in the broadest sense, and this new outlook can be exhilarating. When we are kind and compassionate at home and with our friends and neighbors, our relationships are marked by great beauty, love, and trust, but when we also make humane choices in relation to others outside our circle of friends and family, we actually help to bring peace to our troubled world.

Imagine it's May 1, 2040, and your adult child is reading the newspaper. The headlines include the following:

- Teen activists raise $1 million for local hospital
- Another species recovers from brink of extinction
- Heart disease and cancer rates plummet for tenth consecutive year
- New survey reports young adults "satisfied" or "very satisfied" with lives
- Population stabilizing around globe
- Skirmish ends in peaceful resolution

A generation raised to be humane will create a world where such newspaper headlines are common. Children who learn how to overcome anger and hatred with understanding and commitment to fair resolution create a better world for themselves and others. When they seek truth and live with integrity, all of society benefits. When they are taught to act upon their compassion in creative and thoughtful ways, they are able to discover peaceful solutions to problems.

We all know this is an idealistic vision, but I believe it is within our grasp to raise such children and to create such a world. Although it is not easy to raise humane children in our complex world, there is nothing more important, more meaningful, or, in the end, more fulfilling that we parents can do. Not only will we reap the personal benefits and pleasures of raising such children, we will also be contributing to the creation of a better world for them to inherit.

HOW I CAME TO BELIEVE IN THE VISION OF HUMANE EDUCATION

When I graduated from college in 1983, like many 22-year-olds I wasn't sure what I wanted to do with my life. My liberal arts education prepared me for few careers, and so I spent the next several years at a variety of jobs, pursuing various degrees. Then I serendipitously discovered my life's work. A friend told me about a university summer program for secondary school students. I needed a job, and I could teach (I didn't actually have skills to do much else), and so I called the director of the program and told her I wanted to offer some courses. I got the job. When I taught the young people in my courses about what was happening on our planet and encouraged them to act upon their deepest values, their enthusiasm and commitment to be their best and to help improve the world was so heartening and exciting that I was filled with hope and optimism. I had discovered the power and promise of humane education.

After my second summer teaching these courses, I created a humane education program to take to schools. During one course I taught at a large suburban high school, there was a boy who never cracked a smile or expressed empathy. His name was Mike and he was very bright, but his heart was locked within his tough exterior. He appeared detached and apathetic. I felt that I was not reaching him and that my efforts, at least in his case, were in vain. On the last day of class, a week before Mike would graduate, I decided to lead a Council of all Beings, an activity in which students have the opportunity to become, through their imaginations, another being (whether human, animal, plant or landscape) and to share their thoughts, concerns, and wisdom with the rest of the group. I was a bit apprehensive about doing the Council with Mike and wondered how he would react to such an unusual mode of learning and expression, but my fears were transformed into utter amazement when I heard him speak. During the council he had become the ocean, and speaking as the ocean he raised his voice and addressed the group saying, "My body is crying, and my tears are poison. The life within me is dying, and my heart is broken." I was dumbfounded. Inside this reserved, seemingly dispassionate young man resided a deeply caring poet. When the Council was over, each student made a small promise to do something to help the being for whom he or she had spoken. Mike promised to learn more about ocean ecology, and to stop buying overpackaged and disposable products that he didn't need. Then, as everyone was saying goodbye, he said, "Of all the classes I have taken in high school, this is what I'm going to remember." Whenever I despair that the task of raising humane children in today's world is too great or that the possibility of creating a humane generation is impossible, I think of Mike.

As I continued my work in humane education I began to notice that students who actively endeavored to be humane were more emotionally healthy than their peers who didn't. Not only did their lives increasingly reflect compassion and kindness, they were by and large happier. They may have known more about the problems in our world, but because they were engaged in making a difference, they did not experience the apathy of many of their peers. They tended to be more articulate, more empowered, and more successful at achieving their goals, and they did not suffer from the inner turmoil common among many who know in their heart that they are not living with compassion and integrity.

After several years of offering classes and witnessing the enormous positive effects of humane education, I began to train other people to be humane educators, too, and later co-founded The International Institute for Humane Education (IIHE). IIHE launched the first Humane Education Certificate Program and Master's of Education degree program focusing on humane education in the United States, and we are now seeing comprehensive humane education spread across North America and in many other countries. Humane Education Charter Schools are starting up, and humane education programs are proliferating.

While it's exciting and rewarding to be part of the humane education movement and to help students explore how to live according to their deepest values, something else happened in my life ten years ago that added a whole new dimension to the vision. I became a mother. I realized that I could bring all the skills I had learned as a humane educator to the parenting of my own son and that I could share my knowledge and experience not only with professional teachers, but also with other parents. After all, we parents are our children's first and most important teachers, and we have the most vital and significant task: to nurture and rear the next generation. That realization turned into this book.

BACK TO THE GATHERING OF MOTHERS

After the women had shared their stories and their most fervent hopes for their children, one of them suggested that they help each other with the situations they had discussed. Before they went home to their families, they talked over each problem in detail, offered ideas, reminded one another to be patient, and agreed to come back in a month and talk about what happened when they tried out the suggestions of the group.

This is what transpired: The seven-year-old boy who had played Nintendo all weekend had been asking his mother for his own Nintendo ever since they'd gotten back home. At the suggestion of one of the women in the group, she read up on the effects of video games on the brain. She then sat down with her son and talked about what she noticed happening to him when he played the video game. She mentioned his glazed eyes, his change in behavior and personality, and his inability to divert his attention from the screen, and explained that she didn't think Nintendo was good for him and therefore wouldn't let him get it. She told him how much she loved him and how it was her job to protect him from things that she didn't think were healthy for him. Then she pulled out her old chessboard and gave it to him. It was a beautiful wooden board with intricately carved pieces. Her son had always loved it, and he couldn't quite believe that she would give it to him. "Are you sure?" he asked her. "Yes," she said, "come on, let's play." They got into the habit of playing a game of chess each day when he got home from school, and he stopped asking for Nintendo. "You know," she told the group, "we've really been enjoying each other's company."

The mom whose son had inadvertently learned about pornography used the situation to teach him about the sacredness and beauty of sex, and made his exposure to a perversion of sexuality into an opportunity to share her own values. She was still concerned about how his introduction to pornography might affect him, but she found that having opened the door to discussions about sexuality she was able to talk about love and relationships more easily and was better able to impart her values to her son.

At the suggestion of the group, Sarah's mother, Sharon, planned a weekend trip to visit her own mother, Maria. Maria had been a refugee as a child and had watched her sister and both her parents die. She had never talked much about her past and had become an embittered woman. The group of mothers encouraged Sharon to reach out to her mother, to tell Maria she needed support with Sarah, and to ask Maria to share her life experiences with her granddaughter. They all felt that if Sarah could learn about the suffering of her own grandmother, she might become less self-absorbed and disrespectful. Sharon was nervous asking her mother to talk to Sarah, thinking that she would refuse, but Maria surprised her by saying that if it would help Sharon, she would try to speak the unspeakable. On the four-hour drive to her grandmother's house, Sarah was either complaining or listening to music on her headphones, but on the trip back, Sarah talked to Sharon nonstop about Grandma Maria, about how she'd never understood what had happened to her grandmother, and about how she now could see why her grand-mother was so bitter. She even said to her mother, "It must have been hard growing up with a mom who was so mean and criti-cal." It was the first time in years Sharon could remember Sarah showing her any empathy.

The mom whose daughter would only eat macaroni and cheese and French fries borrowed several whole foods cookbooks from another woman in the group, sat down with her family, and explained that she was going to start cooking in a new and healthier way. All her children balked at the change, but no one wanted to take over the job of food preparation, and when they realized that she was not going to break her resolve they started to eat the new foods. She had to try out a variety of different dishes, and she almost gave up when two of her children com-plained each night and left dinner sitting on their plates, but then she found a couple of recipes that everyone liked and used these as staples while she kept experimenting to find a few more meals that pleased everybody. She also set limits on television watching, and she planned one family outdoor activity each week. Everyone grumbled about this change, too, but the truth was that they had fun, and her overweight daughter actually looked like she had lost a few pounds by the end of the month.

The mother whose son despaired of his broken toys had a good talk with him about what toys he really enjoyed and which ones were made to last. Then he asked her, "Why would anyone make a toy that would break in a few days?" His question sparked a discussion about moneymaking and business ethics, and she was surprised at the wisdom of her young son. Then she talked about the beautiful earth and how it hurt the earth when we made too much garbage. The next thing she knew, her son was trying to figure out how to repair or reuse things rather than throw them out, and she and her family set up a thorough recycling system.

When the women gathered the next month, they had much to share and much to discuss. They had confronted obstacles that had seemed impossible to overcome, and they had made progress. Things weren't perfect, but all the women were enthusiastic about continuing their efforts.

HOW TO USE THIS BOOK

Above All, Be Kind will give you the skills not only to respond effectively to situations like those that confronted the group of mothers above, but also to proactively cultivate the "best qualities of human beings" in your children so that they will grow up to be humane in the broadest sense. But before you can take your children on the journey toward humane living, you must first embark upon the journey yourself. In the first chapter you will be invited to explore humane qualities and to reflect upon whether you are currently embodying them in your own life. Next you will learn specific tools for raising a humane child. There are four elements that come into play when raising children to be humane: providing information; teaching your children to be critical thinkers; instilling the three Rs of reverence, respect, and responsibility; and offering them positive choices. You will also discover how you can use these four elements in your own life to be a better role model for your children, and through a questionnaire you will be able take stock of your life and determine ways in which you would like to change and make more humane choices. The book will explore how to bring the power of example and the tools of raising humane children into play during three developmental stages: the early years, the middle years, and adolescence. *Above All, Be Kind* ends with the inspiring stories of some especially humane young adults. Their lives, stories, and wisdom demonstrate that the promise of raising humane children and creating a humane world can be fulfilled.

ONE

THE BEST QUALITIES OF HUMAN BEINGS

The best, like water,
Benefit all and do not compete ...
In their dwelling, they love the earth;
In their heart, they love what is deep;
In personal relationships, they love kindness;
In their words, they love truth.
In the world, they love peace.
In personal affairs, they love what is right ...

— Lao Tzu

To discover and explore what the word *humane* really implies, I often begin humane education programs by asking the audience, "What do you think are the best qualities of human beings?" I have collected many lists of "best qualities" this way and have been struck by the consistency of the responses. No one has ever answered "Greed" or "Cruelty." No one has said "Bigotry" or "Cowardice." There is uniformity to the responses regardless of the venue and the politics or religion of the person who answers the question. This universality of our view of human goodness resides deep within each of us, whether we identify these values as originating from God, saints, sacred texts, moral inspiration, or simply our own hearts and minds. Having asked the question above to thousands of people, I have compiled the ten most commonly articulated qualities for living a humane life:

1. Willingness to choose and change
2. Kindness
3. Compassion
4. Honesty and trustworthiness
5. Generosity
6. Courage
7. Perseverance, self-discipline and restraint
8. Humor and playfulness
9. Wisdom
10. Integrity

My goal in this chapter is to offer you a vision of what it means to be humane by briefly discussing each of these ten qualities and their importance to a humane life. The stories and quotations in the short essays that follow are meant to offer some concrete examples of what would otherwise remain abstractions. While we all know the definition of these qualities in a general sense, it can be helpful to explore and consider what each looks like in practice. Since you will see the word *humane* repeatedly in this book, I felt it was especially important to discuss each quality separately so that the term *humane* wouldn't simply become an even bigger abstraction. Each time you come across the word *humane*, I'd like you to think of the ten qualities discussed in this chapter *as well as of the qualities you consider to be most important.* These qualities will serve as both your map and destination on the journey toward raising your child to be humane.

1. WILLINGNESS TO CHOOSE AND CHANGE

> *Divine spirit, make me an instrument of peace.*
> *Where there is hatred, let me sow love,*
> *Where there is injury, pardon,*
> *Where there is doubt, faith,*
> *Where there is despair, hope,*
> *Where there is darkness, light,*
> *Where there is sadness, joy ...*
>
> — PRAYER OF ST. FRANCIS

Almost every day of my life I recite the prayer above, and every day of my life I fail to live up to its words. Yet each morning I am reminded that I may choose to be kinder, more compassionate, more loving, and more faithful to my deepest values.

It may seem strange to begin a list of the best qualities of human beings with the concepts of choosing and changing, but in fact the willingness to choose and change is the overarching quality that makes it possible for each of us to become more humane and to raise humane children. Thank goodness we are blessed with the capacity to make new choices.

Viktor Frankl, a Nazi concentration camp survivor, describes choice in this way: "We who lived in concentration camps can remember the men who walked through the huts comforting others, giving away their last piece of bread. They may have been few in number, but they offer sufficient proof that everything can be taken away from a man but one thing: the last of the human freedoms — to choose one's attitude in any given set of circumstances, to choose one's own way."[1]

The ability to choose carries a huge responsibility, yet most of us are barely conscious of our simplest and most frequent choices. From the clothes we put on to the foods we consume, to the ways in which we involve ourselves socially and politically, we are making decisions that affect not only us and our family but also many others. As we learn about the effects of our choices, we can choose more wisely, with more compassion and integrity. In this way, we change ourselves and our lives to better reflect our deepest values. Of all the qualities described in this chapter, it is the willingness to choose and change that gives me the most hope.

2. KINDNESS

"Above all, be kind."

Kindness is the act that makes the virtues discussed in this chapter meaningful. The litmus test for the depth and truth of all these qualities is our response to the following question: Are we being kind? Kindness doesn't mean that we are not strict with our children or direct in our opinions and ideas. The kindest comment, for example, may be the one that is most honest. *Kind* is not synonymous with *nice*. What *kindness* does mean is that we attempt at the deepest and broadest level to assess what does the least harm and the most good in any given situation.

As a child growing up in New York City, I took public transportation to school each day. My parents taught me to give my seat on the bus to elderly or disabled people, but sometimes I just didn't feel like giving up my seat to anyone. When I was tired, I would look down or close my eyes and pretend that I didn't notice the people who needed the seat more than I. But I never felt good about this. I may have remained sitting, but I was never comfortable. When, however, I met another person's eyes and asked with genuine kindness, "Would you like to sit down?" I felt wonderful, and so did they. I remember one time in eighth grade when I was very cranky and irritable but offered my seat to an elderly woman anyway. She thanked me and told me what a kind girl I was. Her words made me feel so good. We started chatting, and my bad mood was completely transformed. That day I learned an important lesson. Kindness is magical. It changes everything.

The power of kindness resides in both its simplicity and its breadth. Not only can we be kind to those with whom we interact, but also to those whose lives we affect, however distantly, through our daily choices. For example, we can make a conscious effort to choose products that are produced humanely and activities that do not cause undue harm to others. What would happen if kindness were to spread in this way? If kindness in our interactions has such tremendous power, what would be unleashed if we began to make kind choices not only toward those in our immediate communities, but also toward those whose lives we affect around the globe?

While it's easy to see the effects of kindness upon our family, friends, and neighbors, it's harder to see how our choices affect others far away from us. Yet once we recognize which choices are kinder, we open the door to a more peaceful and joyful world for everyone. How will you know what the kindest decisions are? By using the tools in this book, you will be able to assess your choices using criteria that will lead you toward ever kinder decisions, and your children will learn how to do this, too. When enough of us practice kindness in this far-reaching way, we will transform the world.

3. COMPASSION

Evoking the presence of the Great Compassion, let us fill our hearts with our own compassion towards ourselves and towards all living beings ...

Let us pray that we ourselves cease to be the cause of suf-
fering to each other.
Let us plead with ourselves to live in a way which will
not deprive other beings of air, water, food, shelter, or
the chance to live ...

— THICH NHAT HANH

Jason was ten years old and loved baseball, but he suffered from both physical and mental disabilities. His father, Bob, wanted to protect him, and so he played catch with him in their back yard and avoided any community games. One day when Bob got home from work and asked Jason if he wanted to play catch, Jason hung his head and said no. When Bob asked him why not, Jason started to cry: "I want to play on a team, Daddy. Why won't you let me play with the other kids?"

Although Bob was worried that Jason might be teased or mocked by the other kids, he knew he had to take the risk, and so he brought Jason to the town field that evening. It turned out there was a game. Bob talked to the coach about Jason, and during the second inning, the coach asked Jason if he wanted to bat. Jason was very excited, and he hurried to get to the plate. Most of the kids on the town team knew Jason from school, but no one from the other team recognized him, although they could see that he was different by the way he moved his body as he ran up to the plate.

Instead of striking him out, the pitcher moved in closer, threw easy underhand balls to Jason, and kept throwing until Jason connected. When Jason finally hit the ball after seven swings, it didn't go far, but the kids who knew Jason started yelling, "Run, Jason! Run!" Their voices were soon joined by those of all the players, on *both* teams. The pitcher deliberately overthrew the ball, and Jason made it to second base. Everyone was cheering. Jason's face glowed as he made it to home plate a few minutes later. He shouted, "I did it Daddy! I did it!" Tears slid down Bob's cheeks as he hugged his joyful son.

Jason's story is not unique. Children are frequently this compassionate if they are raised and encouraged to feel and express their care for others. Compassion is a common emotion, and children feel it all the time. They feel compassion for their family members who are sad, and their friends who are ridiculed. Even a stranded, struggling worm on a sidewalk can elicit compassion. The dictionary defines *compassion* as "a feeling of deep sympathy and sorrow for another who is stricken by suffering or misfortune, accompanied by a strong desire to alleviate the pain or remove its cause." It is one of the most important qualities we can nurture in our children if we want them to be humane.

When we open our hearts, we not only help others, we also increase our own joy. If we allow our compassion to grow, we may find that we have more room in our hearts than we might have realized. We may become more attentive to suffering because we know that compassion has the power to transform and heal.

It's important to make sure that we act upon our compassionate feelings just like the pitcher did in the baseball game. As Edward Abbey has written, "Sentiment without action is the ruin of the soul."[2] Without action, compassion can lead to despair and deep sorrow, but when we do act upon our empathy, not only do we and our children feel empowered and positive about ourselves, our collective acts become an extraordinary force for good.

4. HONESTY AND TRUSTWORTHINESS

The people you have to lie to, own you. The things you have to lie about, own you. When your children see you owned, then they are not your children anymore, they are the children of what owns you. If money owns you, they are the children of money. If your need for pretense and illusion owns you, they are the children of pretense

and illusion. If your fear of loneliness owns you, they are the children of loneliness. If your fear of the truth owns you, they are the children of the fear of the truth.
— MICHAEL VENTURA

When her son was seven, a friend of mine told him he could take his one-dollar allowance out of her wallet. When he came back, she could tell by his odd behavior that he'd taken more than the dollar. She followed him into his room and watched him avert his eyes and giggle, and as she talked to him, she contemplated how to handle the situation. Finally, she calmly asked him if he'd taken more than one dollar from her wallet, and she stressed that the most important thing was that he tell her the truth. He did tell the truth and pulled out another dollar he'd taken. Although she was upset that he'd taken the additional dollar, she was extremely proud of him for telling the truth. She praised him for his honesty and quietly reminded him never to take something that didn't belong to him, from her or anyone else.

Had this mother become angry with her son when he told the truth, she would have taught him a different, and dangerous, lesson. He would have learned that lying could have saved him from trouble. Instead, he learned that honesty was so esteemed by his mother that he was honored for his truthfulness. He will likely continue to be truthful with her, and hopefully with others throughout his life. He already knew it was wrong to steal the extra dollar, but after doing something wrong, he learned that being truthful about misdeeds, making amends, and committing not to do such things again is what can put wrongs right again.

Honesty requires soul-searching. It asks us to lift the veils of protection around us and to be willing to delve inside for the truth about ourselves. If we are lucky, we have friends and family who, with compassion and love, will help us seek the truth. To live with honesty means to acknowledge the whole of our personalities, to recognize when we are inauthentic, and to strive to be more genuine.

Ralph Waldo Emerson wrote, "Every violation of the truth is not only a sort of suicide in the liar, but is a stab at the health of human society."[3] In relation to humane living, honesty means appraising our choices with a willingness to consider whether they truly reflect our values of compassion and kindness. Honesty means we will neither hide from nor rationalize our behaviors, but face ourselves and others truthfully.

Honesty can sometimes be tempered for a greater good, however. Simon Wiesenthal, a survivor of the Nazi concentration camps, tells the story of being called to the deathbed of an S.S. officer who wanted to unburden himself and receive forgiveness for the horrific atrocities he had committed. When the war was over, Mr. Wiesenthal visited the mother of this officer. She was living in rubble, a poor, old woman who lost both her husband and her son in the war. Her son's photo was one of her only possessions and hung on a remaining wall as her greatest treasure. She believed her son to have been a good man. Mr. Wiesenthal chose not to tell the woman the truth about her son. His dishonesty was one of omission. In this case, compassion and honesty were in conflict, and Mr. Wiesenthal chose compassion.

I have a friend whose twelve-year-old daughter, Jill, was faced with a difficult choice about being trustworthy. Jill was spending the weekend with her aunt and uncle and their fourteen-year-old son, Rick. The cousins had always been very close, and Jill adored and admired Rick. When Rick's parents were downstairs watching a movie, Rick told Jill he had something to show her, but she had to promise that she wouldn't tell anyone. She was excited to find out what Rick wanted to show her, and so she agreed. Rick pulled out a bottle of vodka from under his bed and offered Jill a drink. She said, "No thanks," and then watched as Rick drank from the bottle.

When Jill got home the next day she was very agitated. Her parents asked her if anything was wrong, and she said, "No, I'm just tired," and went up to her room. A few hours later she came downstairs and told her parents that she wanted to talk to them. She ended up telling them what happened. She was scared about what her parents would do, and she was worried about losing Rick's trust and friendship. She said to them, "I probably shouldn't have promised not to tell until I knew what I was promising. Are you going to tell Rick's parents?" Jill's mother asked her whether she thought Rick's parents ought to know. "Yeah, I guess so, but Rick is going to hate me."

This story has a good ending. Jill's parents spoke to Rick's parents, and Rick got some much-needed help. Rick also felt terrible about putting Jill into such an awkward and unfair position, and he apologized to her. Jill learned the limits to honesty: being trustworthy does not mean that you should keep a secret if doing so ultimately hurts you or others.

5. GENEROSITY

Americans aren't starving for what they don't have but rather for what they won't give.
— Marianne Williamson

Think of an instance when you gave your time, your money, or your skills to help another. How did you feel? For most of us, generosity brings us joy, deepens our relationships, and contributes to healthy, thriving communities. Yet despite generosity's rewards, giving is not always easy. We wonder if we will have enough for ourselves and our families if we give too freely or generously. Our culture constantly urges us to want more and to keep up with the Joneses. Even if we are rich compared to most people around the world, we may not feel rich when we look at our friends, neighbors, or the affluent characters on television. We may be struggling so hard to meet our mortgage, pay off our credit cards, and get our children everything they want that we feel we have nothing left to give. Yet the more we give, the more we connect with others, and often the fewer material possessions we actually feel we need.

When tragedies strike, and when we can unite around a cause greater than ourselves, we are sometimes able to become generous in ways that we might not have previously imagined. In January 1998, an ice storm struck northern New England, and where I live in Maine thousands of people had no electricity for up to two weeks — no lights, no heat, and no water in the dead of the dark Maine winter. Generosity ran high. People with wood stoves, running water, and electricity opened their homes to strangers. Radio stations broadcast call-in shows in which people offered services and help to others in need.

Generosity is needed all the time, however, not just when calamities strike. Often, we must cultivate generosity and embrace it consciously. I have a friend who actively strives to be generous because generosity is an important value to her. She is a single mother who volunteers frequently at her church, is always willing to cook a meal for someone in need, and gave her car (which she was planning to sell for about $1,000) to a new friend whose vehicle had been totaled in an accident. One spring, her daughter, Annie, wanted to make some money by holding a yard sale. It turned out to be quite successful. My friend was pleasantly surprised when Annie gave every penny to the local food pantry. I suspect that Annie's generosity was influenced by her mother's example.

I know another mother who keeps a box on the kitchen table each year throughout December. The box has a hole in the top, and she regularly puts pocket change or bills into it. At Christmas, the box is sent to a charitable organization. One year, just before Christmas, her six-year-old boy brought out a crisp five-dollar bill, his only one, and put it in the box. She watched her son give a proportionally very large gift to help others and noticed that he delighted in giving! He felt so good about himself when he put his five-dollar bill in the box.

Ebenezer Scrooge, the protagonist in Charles Dickens' *A Christmas Carol*, is a miserably unhappy man until he realizes that what is important in life is not amassing riches, but rather connecting with and helping others. Once Scrooge opens his heart and gives of himself and his wealth, he becomes a happy man. When our children grow up generous in spirit, they, too, are happier. As journalist Cyril Connolly said, "Greed ... is a kind of fear."[4] Conversely, generosity is a kind of freedom.

6. COURAGE

To see what is good and not to do it is want of courage.
— CONFUCIUS

It often takes courage to be humane. The girl who confronts her friends when they are telling racist jokes may face ostracism. The boy who refuses to dissect an animal in biology class may face condemnation, ridicule, and a failing grade. The father who speaks out about industrial pollution in his community may face the wrath of community leaders who are involved with the industry. The mother who is a whistleblower at her job may be fired.

Many people fail to live according to their deepest values because they lack the courage to face the possible negative consequences of their most humane choices. It is easier, and often safer in the short term, to follow the crowd. But living under the tyranny of fear can be a greater burden than following one's truth. Courage does not mean lack of fear. Courageous people choose to persevere despite their fear, to turn fear into an ally that challenges them rather than an enemy that conquers them.

Courageous acts do not have to be obvious displays of bravery. Courage can be quiet and simple. A single parent who raises her children, struggles financially to meet their needs, handles every household repair, every illness, every disaster small or large, and does this alone, with grace and equanimity, demonstrates courage each day.

7. PERSEVERANCE, SELF-DISCIPLINE, AND RESTRAINT

If one advances confidently in the direction of his dreams, and endeavors to live the life which he has imagined, he will meet with a success unexpected in common hours.... If you have built castles in the air, your work need not be lost; that is where they should be. Now put the foundations under them.

— HENRY DAVID THOREAU

When many of us hear the word *perseverance*, what comes to mind is our immigrant ancestors who had to persevere to survive. Success came from hard work and self-discipline. People accepted some deprivation and struggle. The image of the person who achieves the American Dream is a striving pioneer who disciplines himself and perseveres against all odds.

Today U.S. culture does not consistently promote these qualities. We live in a country that encourages immediate gratification more often than perseverance toward difficult or time-consuming goals. Yet when we learn to exercise our will and persevere, we succeed both in achieving our dreams and in building self-confidence.

Instead of encouraging us to restrain our desires, our culture urges us to indulge them. Consider the winter holidays. Rather than promote the deeper meaning of Christmas or Hannukah, or inspire us to give gifts of loving acts or handmade presents, media and advertising exhort us to shop 'til we drop. The passage of time in November and December is measured in "shopping days 'til Christmas," and news reports make holiday buying sound like a patriotic act. Our children may describe their Christmas as merry only if they've received enough presents. Whether or not we can afford such excess, we are relentlessly told to buy. American culture is now marked by debt. Compared to other industrialized countries, we save a tiny proportion of our income, and more people declare bankruptcy every year in the United States than graduate from college.

Perseverance, self-discipline, and restraint are critical to both our individual happiness and our planet's survival. Restraint actually helps us to reach our potential by enabling us to persevere toward our greatest purpose without veering off course. Self-disciplined children often feel safer and calmer than their more undisciplined peers. They know that they can count on and trust themselves. When they learn how to restrain their desires and impulses for a greater good, they discover that they are not at the mercy of every emotion, impulse, or thought.

8. HUMOR AND PLAYFULNESS

Laughter is immeasurable. Be joyful
though you have considered all the facts.
— WENDELL BERRY

Raising our children to be their best means raising them with frequent belly laughs, smiles that last so long they turn into aches, jokes and fun that resound and leave tears of pleasure. We want our children not only to be kind and compassionate, but also to laugh and be playful. This, too, is what it means to be fully human and humane.

Pleasure is sold to us in many ways, and our children are a multi-billion dollar market. Advertising will try to make them want the newest PlayStation, the hundred-dollar pair of sneakers, or the latest Barbie doll, and it will try to make us feel like lousy parents if we don't provide these products for our children. More and more people are realizing that what is meant to bring happiness into their lives isn't fulfilling its promise and is also leaving their children adrift, unable to find true joy.

Potluck suppers, picnics, summer baseball games, and winter sledding — these activities provide the stuff that our children's memories are made of. They offer us and our children the opportunity for humor and play to flourish. When my son hears that we are having friends over for dinner, he is instantly energized and excited. It's true that it's easier to pop a video in the VCR than have another family come over, but when all is said and done, gathering with friends is a huge gift to us and our children. Such gatherings feed our souls and enliven our spirits. We laugh, and we feel connected to others. We build relationships and communities for our children and for ourselves.

9. WISDOM

now the eyes of my eyes are open.
now the ears of my ears awake.

— E.E. CUMMINGS

According to the dictionary, to be wise is to have knowledge about what is true or right, and the judgment to know what action to take. We all know that wisdom is so much more than intelligence. We can be very smart, yet unwise. To be wise requires a commitment to see below the surface, to listen and discern, and to ponder, reflect, and plumb the depths of our own souls for the deepest truth we can find there. Once we have discovered that truth, wisdom requires that we act accordingly. The wise man doesn't simply preach what is right; he makes his life's choices a reflection of his truth.

Many Native Americans speak of the seventh generation. Any significant decisions that the tribe makes must be based on the potential impact to the generations that follow. Imagine if our culture were to make decisions in this way. Would we pollute our air and water or use up our topsoil? Seriously considering the impact of our choices on the seventh generation would overhaul our society. We simply wouldn't persist in many of our current behaviors if we were wise. What if the United States were to cultivate wisdom the way we cultivate individuality, inventiveness, and accomplishment? We would ensure that in our role as the world's leader we were promoting not only the products of our ingenuity, but the wisdom to thrive for generations to come.

10. INTEGRITY

I want to know if you can live in the world with its harsh need to change you. If you can look back with firm eyes saying this is where I stand.

— DAVID WHYTE

Without integrity, practically all of the qualities discussed in this chapter disintegrate. Unless we strive to actually live according to our deepest values, they are meaningless. Integrity is the glue that holds these best qualities together in our lives.

We know when we are not living with integrity, and if we then listen carefully, the dissonance between our values and our actions is audible. While I was writing this book I received a call from a woman raising money on behalf of Human Rights Watch, an organization I'd contributed to for several years. But while I support Human Rights Watch, I don't like telephone solicitations, whether for long-distance phone service, products, or non-profit fundraising, and I told the caller that I would be happy to read their annual appeal, but I did not want to receive phone calls. She assured me I would not be called again, and then proceeded to carry on with her pitch for my support. I interrupted, and asked her to please stop the pitch. She promised me once again that I would not be called in the future, and then continued her script. I raised my voice and said, "You're not listening to me!" Still she continued, until I finally said I would now not give any money to Human Rights Watch, practically shouted goodbye, and hung up.

I couldn't believe it. I wanted to call right back and apologize to this woman who's trying to raise money for a worthy organization and has to endure people like me. True, she didn't listen to me or respect my wishes, but that is no excuse for how badly I behaved and how much I reacted out of anger and took my day's frustrations out on her. I was deeply ashamed of myself. Without integrity we not only hurt others by our lack of effort, will, and commitment, we also hurt ourselves.

Living with integrity requires work. It means that we are actually keeping our commitments and striving to live according to our deepest values. It means that we decide who we want to be and then become that person day by day. It is so important that we teach our children to have integrity because without it, all the other good qualities may disappear in the face of peer pressures or powerful impulses and desires. Integrity will enable our children to remain true to themselves and their own beliefs and values.

HUMANE LIVING: AN ONGOING PROCESS

> *I seek strength not to be greater than my brother or my*
> *sister, but to fight my greatest enemy: myself.*
> — NATIVE AMERICAN WISDOM

If compassion is a birthright, so is apathy. Perseverance competes with laziness. We do not always feel like being kind. Raising our children to be humane does not mean denying or ignoring inhumane feelings. It also does not mean presenting qualities as an either-or dichotomy or as mutually exclusive. We are not either good or bad, persistent or indolent, courageous or cowardly, kind or mean, cruel or compassionate. We contain within us the potential to manifest all of these qualities. What we choose to do with our inhumane impulses is what matters. As Gandalf says to Frodo in *The Lord of the Rings*, "All we have to decide is what to do with the time that is given us."[5]

When we try to live according to our deepest values, and when we teach our children to do likewise, we do so not by denying vices, but by naming them, acknowledging them, discussing them, and choosing not to act on them. As you take on the challenge of embodying and teaching humane values, your children will join you. This process will become your family's personal journey into new and better ways of living and being. What a gift to your children to embark on such a journey! How grateful they will be when they look back upon their childhood and realize that you gave them the inner strength and values to live joyfully, honestly, and with integrity in this world. You will not be perfect, and nor will they, but you will both be traveling on a path toward wholeness and peace. When you look over the list of qualities described in this chapter, again and again you will see that most of them, truly embodied, would dramatically change us, our children, and the world for the better.

ADDITIONAL BEST QUALITIES OF HUMAN BEINGS

In this chapter I have chosen to discuss those qualities that I have seen identified most frequently and persistently, but this list of qualities is by no means complete, nor will it fully represent your personal values. There are so many more qualities that we may embrace, nurture, and teach. Obviously, the concept of "best qualities" is open to interpretation and individual perspective, and in people's answers to the question "What are the best qualities of human beings?" many other virtues are usually mentioned as well. I've included some of them below in the hope that you will find in these qualities more inspiration for your journey:

> humility, creativity, gratitude, tolerance, altruism, patience, forgiveness, curiosity, resilience, forbearance, gentleness, tenderness, attentiveness, spontaneity, commitment, initiative, mindfulness, expressiveness, serenity, flexibility, adaptability, optimism, sensitivity, graciousness, loyalty, mercifulness,

independence, dedication, wonder, passion, appreciation, vibrancy, peacefulness, self-awareness, ingeniousness, equanimity, helpfulness, the ability to rise above circumstances, the willingness to be different, the willingness to reflect.

TWO

TOOLS TO RAISE A HUMANE CHILD: THE FOUR ELEMENTS

If we did the things we are capable of doing, we would literally astound ourselves.

— THOMAS EDISON

JULIA AND YOSHIKO

Julia was about to enter seventh grade when twelve-year-old Yoshiko Fujita emigrated from Japan with her family and moved in next door. Yoshiko barely spoke English, but Julia tried to get to know her anyway, and found that she liked Yoshiko a lot. It was fun to have a neighbor her own age, especially in the summer when she was home most of the time. During the last month of vacation Julia and Yoshiko played together almost every day, and by the time school started they were good friends.

Julia was very popular in her class, although she hadn't always been. When the prettiest girl in fifth grade befriended her, Julia's prestige soared. She'd learned how to stay popular, too. The most important rule was "Don't hang out with unpopular girls."

The first day of seventh grade, the teacher introduced Yoshiko. She was the only new girl in the class, and because she was from Japan and struggled with English, the teacher made a point of saying that the students should make an extra effort to include Yoshiko. She asked Yoshiko to stand up, and Yoshiko's strange accent and averted eyes made some of the students smirk.

Yoshiko wouldn't leave Julia's side, and Julia could tell right away that her friends were not particularly interested in getting to know Yoshiko. It didn't help that Yoshiko wouldn't make eye contact with anyone else. At recess one of the girls in Julia's crowd asked her why she was hanging out with a "Jap." "Got a new friend, Jules?" mocked another girl. Julia responded that she had to be nice because Yoshiko was her new neighbor. "Poor you," said one of the girls in the group. "Yeah, I know," answered Julia.

When Julia got home she was a wreck. She'd betrayed Yoshiko's trust and lied to her friends at school. She didn't know what to do. She couldn't bear the thought of being excluded by the popular girls again, but she also couldn't bear being so mean to Yoshiko. When Julia's mom, Lauren, asked how the first day of school went, Julia said it was horrible. Lauren stopped what she was doing, came over to Julia, and asked her if she wanted to talk about it. Julia told her mom everything that had happened.

Lauren listened to the whole story, and then hugged her daughter. She didn't get angry at Julia for being a bad friend to Yoshiko, but instead said, "You like Yoshiko, don't you?" "Yes," answered Julia, "but I couldn't tell my friends that. And why didn't she even look at anyone else!?" Lauren asked Julia if she recalled meeting the Fujita family when they moved in. "Remember how the whole family seemed very shy at first, Julia? It took a while before they would say hello in the morning when we were out in the yard, or make eye contact. Customs are different in Japan. It can be considered very rude to stare into someone's eyes unless you know them, or to make friendly overtures to strangers."

Julia did remember that it took a while for Yoshiko to warm up to her, but she hadn't paid much attention because she was so outgoing herself that she made up for Yoshiko's shyness by doing most of the talking. Lauren suggested that they walk over to the library and see if they could find any books on Japanese culture. That night, Julia read that in Japan, perhaps because people lived in such close proximity, it was common to respect people's privacy by averting one's eyes in passing.

When Julia was getting into bed, Lauren came in to say goodnight. She asked Julia how she thought Yoshiko's day had been. "It must have been awful. I would've been so embarrassed to stand up in front of a new class like that. She was probably really scared, and then I was mean to her. I hate to think about what she's feeling right now."

"What are you going to do tomorrow, Julia?" Lauren asked her daughter.

"I don't know, Mom. I really don't want to lose my friends, but I'm not going to be mean to Yoshiko. I think I'll introduce her to Shannon. She's nice, and maybe she'll like Yoshiko."

"I think that's a great idea, Julia. I'm proud of you. You know, your real friends will stand by you and your choices."

THE FOUR ELEMENTS

When we read the story above, it doesn't appear that Lauren did all that much to help her daughter, but in fact she utilized what I call the Four Elements. These four elements, which help us raise humane children, are the following:

- Providing information
- Teaching critical thinking
- Instilling reverence, respect, and responsibility
- Offering positive choices

When Julia told her mom about what happened at school, Lauren asked her daughter a few significant questions, offered some comments and suggested that they learn some more about Japanese culture. In this way, Lauren provided information and taught her daughter to think critically about why Yoshiko might have acted the way she did. Next, Lauren invited her daughter to think about Yoshiko's feelings, inspiring Julia's compassion and respect for Yoshiko. Lastly, she asked Julia what she would do the next day, offering her daughter an opportunity to reflect upon the upcoming choices she would face when she went to school in the morning and to take responsibility for her actions. Lauren didn't actually need to tell her daughter what the best choice might be because Julia figured that out for herself. These four elements, offered in a relatively simple fashion, helped Julia to deal with a difficult situation and make a humane decision.

Although modeling humane values and humane choices will be the primary way in which you raise your child to be humane, the Four Elements provide important tools that parents can use to help their children embody the positive qualities described in Chapter 1. They are the same tools that we humane educators use in classrooms, but of course anyone can use them. There's nothing mysterious or complicated about the Four Elements. We all use these tools. But it's when we put them together *consciously* that they become such a powerful method for change and positive choices in our lives.

ELEMENT 1: PROVIDING INFORMATION

What information do you want your children to have? It is worth pausing for a moment to really consider your answer to this simple question. Many of us don't think about this question very often, deferring instead to the wisdom of our culture, our teachers, and our school boards to impart essential information and skills to the next generation. But schools aren't primarily designed to teach children to be humane. In fact, recent school reforms have resulted in less time spent on citizenship and more time spent on preparation for tests. If you want to raise compassionate children, they will need information that is not generally offered to them in their schools or through the media.

Teachers seldom teach children about the origins of their cultural values, the effects of media and advertising on their desires and behaviors, or the ways in which societal values influence individuals. Nor are children commonly taught where their clothes or food comes from, how the products they use are made, where their trash goes, how their electricity is produced, or what effects common chemicals have on the environment. Children are not even always taught basic information about the ecology that underpins their lives. Yet in order to actually live a humane life, we must have such information so that we can make humane choices.

To provide information for your children, you must first gather it yourself. Lauren happened to know a bit about Japanese culture so that she could help her daughter think critically about what happened at school, but she also suggested that they head to the library to learn more. Gathering information can be an exciting adventure in which you get to learn and grow as you help your child learn and grow. Collecting information for your children does not mean that you pore over texts each night, but rather that you consider what is most important to you, cultivate your inquisitiveness, seek out knowledge, and then enjoy the process of learning. It also means that you bring an attitude of openness to situations so that you are ready and able to seek out the information you need to address events as they arise. Once you have new information in hand, you can share it with your child.

Information gathering can become a family adventure, too. It's quite eye-opening to tour the city reservoir or sewage treatment plant, to visit the local nursing home to discover how care is provided to elderly citizens, to go to farms that produce your food, to take a trip to the company that supplies electricity to your home, or to explore the factories that make the products you use. Most of us are so disconnected from the realities behind the basic services and products that allow us to live our lives. If we don't have this kind of fundamental knowledge, our ability to make wise choices is impaired. By discovering this information, you pave the way for more conscious decision-making and more compassionate and aware living.

You may find that as your children get older you will begin to gather other sorts of information together, too. Trips to libraries, attending talks in your community, reading pertinent magazines and newsletters, doing Internet searches, sharing articles and fact sheets, or writing to organizations and corporations to request information can all become family activities that build your relationships while increasing both your knowledge base and information gathering abilities. The skill of information gathering is one that will be of great value to your child over the course of her life. As you learn how to use this first of the Four Elements, you will be opening your child's mind and helping her become a lifelong learner. Armed with information, your child will also have the basics for the next element: critical thinking.

ELEMENT 2: TEACHING CRITICAL THINKING

Providing information is only the first step — teaching your children to assess that information is crucial. Without the ability to think critically, we are all susceptible to distortions and lies that are presented as facts, and to propaganda disguised as truth. Once we have gathered and provided information, we then need to teach our children how to become critical thinkers and how to examine for themselves whether the information is true. As hard as you may have worked to gather information for your child, now it's time to ask your child to be critical of it.

When I visit a school to offer a humane education program, I often tell the students that I do not want them to believe me. They are usually shocked when I say this. They are not used to teachers telling them to be skeptical of the information the teachers themselves are imparting. But I want students to question me in order to discover the truth for themselves. In this way they'll learn how to question everything, whether it comes from government sources, corporations, the nonprofit sector, the media, public relations firms, the left, the right, or in between. I am not trying to create cynics who don't trust anyone or anything, but rather thinkers who are able to sort through many fragments and shards of truth, assess accuracy, and come to reasonable and reliable conclusions. To do this I may show students video footage taken during undercover investigations of certain companies and contrast it with information from those companies' public relations firms. I may bring in advertisements to analyze, or pamphlets from various corporations and nonprofit organizations. I lead activities that require students to sort through contradictory and inconsistent messages in order to awaken their own ability to discern truth. Teaching children to be critical thinkers can also be as simple as asking them to think hard about a situation rather than make snap judgments. Lauren helped Julia think critically by asking her to remember how the Fujita family first behaved when they moved in next door, and by then encouraging her to consider why they might have acted differently from a typical American family.

My favorite critical thinking activity involves playacting the role of an alien who is visiting planet Earth. The alien, whom I call Zenobia, travels through the universe on a fact-finding mission to learn what other beings and other cultures believe and do. It is very important to Zenobia that she not offend anybody during her visits to various planets, so she is anxious to learn appropriate behaviors in each locale. When she is on Earth, Zenobia particularly likes to visit ten- to thirteen-year-olds because they are very forthright in answering her questions. Because Zenobia is from such a distant solar system, she travels noncorporeally, and occupies my body while she is in the classroom, speaking and hearing through me. Usually, I close my eyes to let Zenobia appear, and when I open my eyes, it is she who speaks to the class. The children are delighted by this game and by the opportunity to teach someone who is utterly ignorant about their world.

Zenobia asks the students a series of questions about how, in their culture, they are supposed to treat others. She asks about how they're supposed to treat elderly people and people with disabilities, and about how they're supposed to treat people with a different skin color or religion. "We're supposed to treat them with respect," the children respond. "Is it ever okay to harm someone because they have a different skin color?" she asks. "No, but some people do," answer the students. "Why?" asks Zenobia, and the children pause as they try to figure out how to explain racism. "What about eye color? Is that important?" Zenobia asks. The students laugh. "How could anyone think eye color matters?" they say before realizing that skin color is equally arbitrary. Zenobia quickly discovers that the values of compassion and care that the students first articulate are contradicted by such realities as war, slavery, and prejudices of all kinds. Zenobia is always confused, and the students begin scratching their heads as well.

Zenobia also asks the students about how they are supposed to treat other species on their planet, such as birds. At first, students usually respond that we should respect them, but some student will fairly quickly point out that we eat chickens and turkeys and hunt certain birds for recreation. Zenobia might ask about dogs and pigs, and discover other inconsistencies that surprise her. "Why do you eat pigs, but not dogs?" she asks. Some bright student will usually let Zenobia know that in some countries people do eat dogs, and in some cultures people don't eat pigs. "What is the difference?" asks Zenobia, and the conversation about our inconsistent treatment of animals begins.

Whenever I play the role of Zenobia in a classroom, it is as if I can actually see light bulbs going on in students' brains. They are thinking about concepts they haven't considered before, and the excitement (as well as the confusion) in the room is often palpable. What we profess and what we do in our culture is often contradictory and perplexing, based on tradition, habit, and marketing rather than on deeply considered values. For example, many children are raised with the religious commandment, "Thou shalt not kill," yet their country supports the death penalty. Many are taught to treat animals humanely, but laws against cruelty do not apply to farmed animals, only to those considered to be pets. Many are taught not to waste, yet disposable products are the norm.

Young people often remember Zenobia years after they have "met" her. Once when I was walking down a school hallway, not having visited that particular school in a couple of years, a student came up to me and said, "Hey, aren't you that alien woman? What's her name? Zenobia?" This boy had only seen me during a brief visit to his classroom two years earlier, yet he remembered Zenobia. She wore no mask, was not in costume, spoke to the class only through me, a visiting humane educator, yet she was memorable. I think the reason children remember Zenobia is that she makes them think and grapple with ideas well beyond the confines of the school walls.

Parents do not have to play the role of Zenobia to teach their children to be critical thinkers, but the example of Zenobia illustrates the ways in which we can cultivate critical thinking in ourselves as parents as well as in our children. Becoming a critical thinker means bringing both curiosity and a healthy dose of skepticism to all information, listening to many points of view, asking questions, and believing nothing until it has become true for you. It means learning how to discern fact from opinion and bringing a scientist's inquiring mind to life. Raising a child to be a critical thinker means encouraging her to ask questions and seek out answers. It means that when your child asks you, "Why does God allow bad things to happen to good people?" or "Why is it okay to kill people in wars?" or "Why do some people not like other people because of what country they're from?" or a host of other very perplexing and important questions, you do not respond with pat answers but rather invite your child to grapple with these questions with you. Even when your child asks a simple question such as, "Who made those tracks in the snow?" you can resist the impulse to simply provide the answer and instead respond, "That's a good question — what do you notice about the tracks?" This is not to say that we should not answer our children's factual questions or offer our opinions, but rather that we cultivate their ability to analyze and explore for themselves before we stifle their creative thinking with what we think is the right answer.

Raising our children to be critical thinkers also means that we ask them questions like Zenobia does. If our teenage son and daughter are watching TV, we can watch with them. When commercials come on, we can encourage our children to analyze them. We can ask, "Why do you think the perfume commercial is a short story about falling in love?" or "How did you feel watching the beer ad? Did it make you want to drink beer? How come?" If we're watching the local news with our adolescents, we can teach them how to look carefully for public relations videos disguised as news. More and more TV stations are using what are called Video News Releases (VNRs) to fill in air time. VNRs are paid for by corporations — such as pharmaceutical, coal, oil, or timber companies — that want to promote their products. They are provided free of charge to news stations. If you see a report promoting a new breakthrough in health care, for example, featuring nonlocal footage in a laboratory, there's a good chance you're watching a commercial disguised as news. By learning how to recognize such advertising and teaching your teenager to do likewise, you help build critical thinking skills.

If we teach our children critical thinking, then instead of blindly believing all the messages they receive, they will learn to ask questions and find out what is true through investigation, research, and thought. I'm not suggesting that our children will be looking at their lives as an ongoing research project, but rather that this attitude of critical thinking will become integrated into how they interact with the world. They will be able to make humane choices because they will have both the knowledge and discernment to make wise decisions.

ELEMENT 3: INSTILLING REVERENCE, RESPECT AND RESPONSIBILITY

While it is crucial to have knowledge and the power to think critically, without the three Rs of reverence, respect, and responsibility, our ability to become fully humane is limited. If the traditional three Rs (reading, writing, and arithmetic) are the basics that we want our children to master academically, then reverence, respect, and responsibility are the three Rs that our children need to master for the sake of their souls and the health of the world. Reverence is an *emotion* that we can nurture in our very young children, respect is an *attitude* that we instill in our children as they become school-agers, and responsibility is an *act* that we inspire in our children as they grow through the middle years and become adolescents. The following story illustrates how the three Rs can be nurtured in a young person.

JOSEPH AND MARCUS

Joseph grew up in the mountains of North Carolina and spent much of his childhood roaming the woods, playing in brooks, and climbing mountains in the southern Appalachians. When he grew up, there were few job opportunities in his rural hometown, and so he moved to Philadelphia to find work. He got a job in a factory, eventually became a machinist, married Selena, a Philadelphia native, and settled into a working-class neighborhood in the heart of the city.

When their oldest son, Marcus, was eleven, Joseph realized how little his boy knew about nature and how few opportunities Marcus had to enjoy the outdoors. Marcus' school was surrounded by concrete sidewalks and brick buildings, crack vials littered the streets, and the only wildlife were the few pigeons who nested on building ledges.

Joseph decided that he wanted to find some way to introduce Marcus to the natural world. Philadelphia has one of the largest urban parks in the United States with miles of trails along the Wissahickon Creek. Joseph knew about the Wissahickon woods but had never been there. He didn't have a car, and it seemed complicated to get to the park even though it was only ten miles away. Joseph called SEPTA, the Philadelphia area public transportation system, and found out that there were a few ways that he could get to within one mile of the Wissahickon woods.

It was a warm Saturday at the end of May when Joseph told Marcus he was going to take him on a special trip. They packed sandwiches, crackers, apples, and water bottles into Marcus' school backpack, took two buses and a train, and walked twenty minutes before they arrived at one of the many Wissahickon trailheads. "Which way do you want to go, Marcus?" Joseph asked his son. "You want *me* to choose?" Marcus responded, surprised and a little anxious.

There were three paths: one went up a hill into dark woods on the left, one snaked through some brambles to the right, and the largest path went straight ahead through the woods down a hill. Marcus was nervous about the whole trip, and so he chose the widest, most well-traveled path. They walked down the hill, huge trees towering over them, sunlight dancing on the forest floor as the wind rustled the leaves overhead. In about ten minutes, they reached the Wissahickon Creek. Joseph noticed that the brownish-yellow water smelled rank, but Marcus didn't seem to realize that the creek was anything but magnificent. There were ducks floating on the water, and Marcus whooped with excitement. Joseph suggested they throw the ducks some bits of crackers, and Marcus was amazed that they swam over immediately and got so close to him. He marveled at the iridescent green feathers on the male mallard's neck and the shiny purple color almost hidden among the brown feathers of the females. They broke their crackers into tiny pieces and fed the ducks until there were no crackers left. Then Joseph taught Marcus how to skip stones along the water. Marcus was amazed at how many times the stones could bounce along the surface of the water when his dad threw them.

At the end of the day, Marcus asked his dad if they could come back again, and Joseph said they would. It had been such a wonderful day, and Marcus talked nonstop at dinner, telling his mother all about the ducks and the stones and the forest. Joseph decided that he would try to take his son to the park every Saturday. The next weekend, Marcus chose the path through the brambles. It turned out the brambles were wineberry bushes and they were in bud. Joseph told Marcus that in about six weeks, the berries would be ripe. "We have to come back then. Okay, Dad?"

The air was perfumed with wild roses and honeysuckle, nonnative plants that had taken over portions of the woods. Marcus didn't know that the plants didn't really belong in these woods; all he knew was that he'd never smelled anything so good in his life. As they were walking, Marcus saw someone move swiftly into a grove of trees in a valley just below him. It was a deer! In fact, there were five deer, almost invisible against the brown leaves on the ground. Marcus had never seen a deer before, and he couldn't believe how beautiful they were. He watched one large female who stood like a statue. Her eyes were enormous, and she was close enough that he could even see her long eyelashes. She stared at him for what seemed like forever before snorting, lifting her tail, and leaping away in a flash. Marcus was speechless.

All week long Marcus looked forward to his trips to the Wissahickon. He and Joseph discovered wild grapes, snakes of poison ivy climbing up trees, sassafras and spice bushes, tulip tree flowers scattered on the forest floor, and a fox den. One afternoon it was so hot that Marcus asked his father if they could swim in the creek, but Joseph told his son that the water was too polluted. Then Joseph began to tell Marcus stories about the Appalachian woods of his childhood, about how he swam all summer long in creeks and rivers and how the water was actually clean enough to drink. Marcus said he couldn't imagine drinking from a creek, and Joseph told his son that when he was young, no one could have imagined that the creeks would be so poisoned that you *couldn't* drink from them. "I would've thought you were crazy if you told me all the creeks would be too polluted to drink from by the time I grew up," Joseph said. Marcus wanted to know what they could do to clean up the Wissahickon creek so they could swim in it. He asked his dad what exactly made the water unsafe for swimming and where the pollution came from. Joseph didn't know the answers to these questions but suggested that he and Marcus could do some research and find out.

When they first started going to the Wissahickon woods, Marcus noticed that his dad sometimes picked up trash and put it in his pocket to throw out later, but there was a lot of trash, so one day Marcus suggested that they bring a plastic bag with them. They got in the habit of making sure that the path was free of trash wherever they walked. When they saw some teenagers littering one day, Joseph offered them a plastic bag and asked them to please make sure that they didn't leave trash in the woods. They seemed irritated, but also somewhat embarrassed, and said they'd clean up.

Joseph loved his weekend outings with Marcus, but he also wanted Marcus to have more opportunities to be outdoors. He decided to talk to a few neighbors on their block to see if anyone wanted to create a community garden in the small lot between two brick houses. The lot was littered with glass, and the soil was hard and compacted, but there were several families in the neighborhood that thought creating a garden was a great idea. Summer had just begun, and there was a lot of work to do. Marcus and a few other kids worked hard with several adults on the block to transform the hard dirt into fertile soil.

By the beginning of July the soil was finally ready for planting. It was already late in the season to be planting seeds, but some crops, like radishes, herbs and flowers, did just fine. One of the neighbors with a car offered to drive to a nursery, and so they were able to buy tomatoes and basil and a few other seedlings that hadn't sold earlier in the season. They also planted some collards that would be ready in the fall, and planned to plant a late summer crop of lettuces.

Marcus paid close attention to the weather, watering the garden when there was little rain. He weeded and mulched and turned the compost pile with a shovel, but his favorite thing to do was to head to the garden before dinner each night and gather some herbs, vegetables and flowers. Every day when Joseph got home from work, he joined Marcus, praised his work, and helped him with his gardening tasks. After dinner they carried their food scraps to the compost pile. Marcus loved the time he was spending with his dad. He was happier than he'd ever been in his life.

Reverence

Reverence invites us to feel deeply and intimately a profound appreciation for the world, for its people, its animals, its beauty, its mystery, and its complexity. To feel reverence is to experience wonder and awe. It is a powerful emotion that helps foster such qualities as compassion, patience, love, kindness, perseverance, restraint, and honesty. When we are deeply reverent, our actions become an expression of this powerful emotion. When Joseph took Marcus to the woods, Marcus experienced a profound reverence for the life around him, for the ducks and deer, for the trees and plants, and also for the very days themselves. He felt reverence for his father and for the time they spent together.

From the moment of birth reverence is one of the most important and abiding gifts we can nurture in our child. If we help our children to revere what is most worthy, we will pave the way for them to later show respect and take responsibility. There is a Vietnamese saying, "When eating a fruit, think of the person who planted the tree." Living in such a way that we dwell for even a moment on others who make our life possible, on the miracle of life itself, on the wonder of the air, the water, and the fruits of our earth, is living with reverence. What we revere we protect and honor. When a small child feels reverence for goodness, for nature, for the diversity of life, for individual rights, she will likely grow up to be humane because that reverence will again and again lead her toward compassionate choices and humane living.

Abraham Heschel wrote, "We can never sneer at the stars, mock the dawn or scoff at the totality of being. Sublime grandeur evokes unhesitating, unflinching awe."[1] I agree with Rabbi Heschel, but I also know that we can fail to look at the stars, to witness the dawn, or to consider the totality of being, and so diminish our opportunities for awe. Growing up in New York City, I rarely saw the stars at night or experienced the breathtaking promise of dawn. Instead I saw thousands of early morning cartoons and the neon glamour of a Manhattan night. That I grew to experience awe and reverence for the earth and the mystery of life attests to the yearning and capacity we all have within us to feel reverence. No matter where we live, there are opportunities to watch a sunrise or a sunset or to dwell upon the wonder of existence. Joseph found a way to bring Marcus into the woods despite the fact that they lived several bus trips, a train ride, and a mile-long walk away.

Reverence is a fragile feeling, easily damaged by cynicism, ridicule, or the false appearance of sophistication. Our society too easily shatters reverence with its materialistic values and crude or shocking images. Our culture today offers children fewer and fewer opportunities to experience reverence. In many neighborhoods it is too dangerous to allow children to play outdoors by themselves, and so these children sit in front of the television. The more they sit in front of the television, the more commercials will shape their desires. The more their friends and classmates sit in front of the television, the more their peer culture will revolve around commercial values. Video and computer games perpetuate the cycle of separation from world of nature and relationships. We live in an era in which our children's leisure time, play time, and imaginative time have become saturated with screen images and media values.

More than ever before it is critical that parents actively commit to nurturing reverence for this earth and its myriad creatures, for the best qualities in human beings, and for the mysterious unknown. What is so wonderful about making this commitment to bring reverence to your child is that it will renew your own reverence. It wasn't only Marcus who benefited from the trips to the Wissahickon woods. Joseph's reverence was rekindled, he more deeply connected with his son, and he remembered the stories of his childhood that he was able to share with Marcus.

Respect

Respect is reverence turned from an emotion into an attitude towards others. We don't just feel respect, we show it. As our children grow up, we can, while still nurturing reverence, move toward instilling respect. We do this in part by showing respect to them and in part by demonstrating what it means to have respect for others. Promoting respect in our children may mean turning off the television if the programs they are watching model disrespect; it may mean demonstrating respect for our environment and community by good citizenship; it may mean teaching our children to be polite; or it may mean that when they are young, we encourage play dates with children who are respectful so that peer influences support our values as parents.

If we are successful at nurturing our children's feelings of reverence, then respect will follow fairly naturally. If children have reverence for the earth, showing respect will mean that they won't cause undue or unnecessary destruction. If they have reverence for the good in human beings, showing respect will mean that they will not only be polite and considerate but also try diligently not to participate in human exploitation by consciously choosing which products to buy and which ones not to buy. If they have reverence for other species, showing respect will mean that they won't destroy or pollute animal habitats or knowingly participate in cruelty. Although Joseph modeled respect for Marcus by picking up trash on their outings, it was Marcus who suggested they bring a plastic bag to take that respect one step further. His reverence for the woods led him to want to show respect by keeping the forest free from garbage.

Although reverence is terribly important and will naturally lead to respect, reverence is not a prerequisite for respectful behavior. For the sake of peace, we must all bring an attitude of respect to our interactions, regardless of whether we feel reverence. This "hands-off" respect will prevent us from harming others despite impulses that might threaten to break our resolve. One does not have to have esteem for (or even like) someone to show that person respect; we do not have to have reverence for rivers to refrain from polluting them, nor do we have to venerate other species to respect their right to exist free from human abuse. This being said, it is much easier to promote respectful attitudes and behaviors among children who feel compassion, wonder, and awe. Marcus' respect followed naturally from his love of the park. Although Joseph could have taught Marcus not to litter or to pick up trash on the sidewalk where they lived, Marcus' own inclination first to emulate his father and then to take his father's example one step further grew out of his own reverence for nature.

Responsibility

To be responsible means to be answerable for our actions. As our children move through the middle years of childhood and approach adolescence, it is important to invest them with more responsibilities so that they learn how to become mature, independent, accountable citizens who put their humane values into concrete actions. Although Joseph did not consciously set out to teach his son responsibility, Marcus became a more responsible boy in the span of a few months. When Joseph brought together neighbors to create a community garden, Marcus was invited to be part of an important project. His reverence for nature and his respect for the environment naturally led to responsibility. Although only eleven years old, Marcus was demonstrating that he could be responsible for certain tasks such as watering, weeding, and helping with the compost. Every day, Joseph joined his son after work, supporting Marcus with words of appreciation.

Marcus also learned to take responsibility for solving problems. When he found out that the creek he loved was too dirty to swim in, Marcus wanted to do something about that pollution. Although he was still young, he wished to become involved in restoring the creek, and he was willing to take some responsibility for pursuing that dream. While it wasn't his fault that the creek was polluted, his reverence and respect were leading him toward a sense of communal responsibility to improve the creek. He felt empowered to make a difference. He believed that cleaning up the creek wasn't solely up to him but that he could be part of something positive. Instead of thinking, "I didn't do it, so I don't need to do anything about it," Marcus thought, "I didn't do it, but I can help change it because I want to swim here." Who knows what Marcus will grow up to do. Perhaps he'll volunteer in the park during high school. Perhaps he will become Philadelphia's next Park Commissioner. Whatever Marcus does in his future, however, he carries with him powerful feelings of reverence, an attitude of respect, and a burgeoning sense of responsibility. These three Rs will surely be as valuable in his life as reading, writing, and arithmetic.

ELEMENT 4: OFFERING POSITIVE CHOICES

It is the last of the Four Elements that makes the first three meaningful. It's not enough to have information and the ability to think critically and to deeply feel reverence and respect. We must also be empowered and able to make responsible, positive choices. We would feel very differently about Lauren's success at helping her daughter if Julia went back to school and snubbed Yoshiko. It is because Julia had a positive plan of action that we feel good about the story.

While it's important to help our children become critical thinkers who have important information at their disposal and while it's crucial that they are able to feel compassion and reverence, they are at the mercy of despair and anger if we leave them without healthy and humane choices.

Imagine that your fifth grader has just heard a radio report about sweatshops and has learned that her brand of sneakers was manufactured using sweatshop labor. Your daughter had never known that people who made her shoes were so deprived and mistreated, and she comes to you quite distressed. She begins to ask you questions about whether the pay the sweatshop workers receive is enough to live on and whether the workers would be worse off without those jobs. She expresses tremendous compassion and concern for these people halfway around the globe and tearfully asks you, "What can we do?" Now imagine that your child is left with no choices, nothing to do to change such exploitation or to make a difference. What would be the consequences of feeling a lack of alternatives?

Without positive choices, we pave the way for apathy. If our children learn about factory farming and the realities behind their fast food hamburger but are offered no alternatives, they may begin to feel impotent. If they love the earth and learn about the dangers to our planet, they may feel despondency and despair if we leave them without hope for change. If, however, we help our children to discover ways to make a difference and help improve the world, we empower them to become humane people.

At this point you may be thinking that your best choice might be to keep depressing information from your child rather than run the risk of raising an apathetic cynic, but your children will eventually learn about the suffering and destruction in the world. While it's very important to protect your children from the realities of cruelty and exploitation when they are young, as they get older it is far better that they learn information from and with you, that you nurture their empathy, and that you join them in the search for humane choices rather than that they be bombarded with discouraging news without your involvement in promoting positive solutions. The truth is that many pre-teens and adolescents are already cynics. They know about the threats to the ecosystem and the suffering of other people and other species. Deep down most of them know that materialism is not ultimately satisfying or sustainable and that the latest trends don't amount to much, but they often don't realize that they have choices that can make a difference in their own lives and in the lives of others. Their cynicism may have turned into apathy, their despair into self-destructive behavior.

The answer, then, is not to hide difficult truths from our preteen and adolescent children but rather to engage the power of their minds and hearts toward becoming part of the solution. The answer is to seek out and encourage our children to come up with humane choices in the face of an often inhumane world.

SUMMARY OF THE FOUR ELEMENTS

This introduction to the Four Elements is meant to serve as a framework for teaching humane values to your children. You can periodically ask yourself the following questions regarding these four elements:

1. Am I seeking out and providing important information to my child?
2. Am I teaching my child to think critically?
3. Am I nurturing reverence, inspiring respect, and instilling responsibility in age-appropriate ways?
4. Does my child understand that she has choices to improve herself and the world?

While it might initially sound challenging to learn how to use the Four Elements, you will discover that this framework can become as natural as Lauren's response to Julia. In Chapters 4, 5, and 6, you'll learn how to use these four elements during the different stages of your child's life, but first, in the next chapter, you'll find out how to use them yourself in order to make more humane choices and become the best role model you can be.

THREE

YOUR LIFE IS YOUR MESSAGE

It is possible to kill a million people without personally shedding a drop of blood. It is possible to destroy a culture without being aware of its existence. It is possible to commit genocide or ecocide from the comfort of one's living room.

— DERRICK JENSEN

MAHATMA GANDHI WAS ONCE ASKED BY A REPORTER, "What is your message?" He answered, "My life is my message." When I first heard about this response, I was struck by its truth and universality. I realized that my life was my message, too, and that nothing I said mattered very much if I wasn't making sure that my life reflected my values. Gandhi had been a hero of mine for many years. His courage, self-discipline, and compassion had always been profoundly inspirational to me, yet the simple words "My life is my message" have become more significant to me as a guide for humane living than any of his heroic acts or compelling speeches. These five words are also terribly humbling. When I make an inhumane choice or treat someone with disrespect, I hear the echo of Gandhi's words and realize that my life is not always the message I want it to be.

More than anything you will ever say to your children, your *life* — the choices you make and the values you embody — will be their biggest teacher. In order to raise our children to be humane, we parents must become good role models for them. If only it were so easy! Even though I have made it my life's work to learn and teach about humane living, every day I face my own lack of integrity, compassion, and will. For example, I yell at my son, Forest, far too often. Even ten minutes after meditating on peace and compassion, I've been known to rant about his messy room. For that matter, I've snapped at him for interrupting me while I'm meditating! I want so much to be consistently kind to Forest, not only because I love him but also because I know that the more I actually model kindness and respect, the more he will come to embody these qualities himself. Nonetheless I often fail to model the message I most want to convey.

Then there are the many occasions when I don't make the kindest choices in relation to others outside of my family and community. For instance, over the past decade I've become more and more committed to buying the bulk of my clothes at thrift shops because I want to recycle used materials rather than contribute to the production of more stuff. But periodically some glossy catalog arrives in my mailbox. Most of the time I put it in the recycling bin and call the company to request that my name be removed from its mailing list. But some days I open the catalog and start turning the pages. The next thing I know I'm ordering something that I don't really need, that's made with nonorganic cotton, and that may have been produced in a sweatshop.

I tell you these stories because I want you to know that I know it's not easy to always be kind — whether at home with your family or in relation to the earth, other people, or other species. I realize how difficult it is to scrutinize one's choices and hold up a mirror to one's actions, and I'm very aware of the fact that each of us will be faced with emotions and circumstances that compete with our desire to make the most humane choices. Sometimes frustration or anger will stand in the way of our kindness, as in the case when we are not as patient and compassionate toward our children as we might want to be. Sometimes desires will eclipse our deeper values, and we will make decisions to enhance our own pleasure, possibly at someone else's expense.

Choosing to be kind takes effort and work, but so much good comes from this work. In his novel *Heart of Darkness*, Joseph Conrad wrote, "I don't like work ... but I like what is in the work — the chance to find yourself."[1] When you work at modeling humane values, you will not only find yourself, you will also help your children and the world. Each time you make a choice that is a bit kinder, you show your children how to be humane, and they in turn learn from the message of your life. The task before each of us is to choose compassion in the face of apathy that deadens our spirit, restraint in the face of desires that can harm, and courage in the face of fears that hold us back — and to do so in practical, concrete ways that translate our ethics into action. We will not always make the kindest choice, but by staying aware and remaining committed to making our life the message we want it to be, we'll be able to make kinder choices more and more often.

It's fairly obvious when we are not being kind to our children. What's much harder to discern is when our choices are indirectly harming others farther removed from us. Usually the effects of our choices on other people, other species, and the earth are hidden from view. But to be humane means not only to be kind and considerate within our family and community, but also to live our lives so that we minimize suffering for our distant neighbors. It includes not only being loving toward the family dog or cat but also learning to live a life that is not cruel to any animal; not only respecting our personal home environment but also discovering how to diminish the harm we cause to the planetary environment, our ultimate home.

This chapter is intended to provide you with the tools to apply the virtues described in Chapter 1 outside the walls of your home so that you can model humane values more fully and consistently. It is this expansive practice of humane qualities that will really improve the world your children will inherit and provide an ever more meaningful model for them to emulate. In the chapters that follow I will return to the ways in which you can raise your child to be kinder and more compassionate in their interactions with their family and friends, but because the vision of raising humane children is potentially so transformative, I will lay the groundwork here for modeling a compassionate life in a far-reaching way. This chapter will also offer suggestions for building community around shared values so that your message will be reinforced, and your children will be surrounded by people who are striving to live and model a humane life in the broadest sense.

EXPANDING HUMANE VALUES TO INCLUDE EVERYONE

Below are some choices that we each make that can have an impact not only on ourselves and our children but also on others outside of our family:

- Choices about what our family wears
- Choices about what our family eats
- Choices about what kinds of entertainments we choose
- Choices about our vehicle(s)
- Choices about our homes, furniture, remodeling, and household repairs
- Choices about toys
- Choices about personal care and cleaning products

Hearing that these choices affect others, however, doesn't really help us make kinder decisions. In order to make humane choices, we need knowledge that most of us just don't have. We simply can't tell whether any given production process caused harm to someone far away from us unless we have information that is not generally offered to us on product labels. For example, unless a product label clearly states that during the production process, no sweatshop labor was used, no animals were caused to suffer, and no environmental pollution took place, we cannot know who or what might have been harmed. It's beyond the scope of this book, however, to provide the detailed information each of us would need to make the most compassionate choices. Instead, this chapter will teach you how to use the Four Elements described in Chapter 2 as a method to assess *any* choice. In addition to explaining how to use the Four Elements in your personal decision-making, this chapter also includes several information boxes (starting on the next page) that provide statistics or background facts about a few of the issues which are important to understand in order to make kinder choices. These "Did you know?" facts and statistics are followed by "Let Kindness Grow" information that offers positive solutions and alternatives. You'll find more information in the Helpful Hints section at the end of the book. However, both the information boxes and the Helpful Hints only touch upon a few issues briefly. It's my hope that this small bit of knowledge will spur you on to learn more.

DID YOU KNOW THIS ABOUT CLOTHES?

- Most clothes sold in America are produced overseas, and many of them are made in sweatshops. Sweatshop workers, some of whom are children, spend up to 14 hours a day working in extremely unhealthy conditions. Pregnant women are routinely fired. Sweatshop workers are not paid a living wage, yet because of rampant poverty and limited options they have few, if any, choices about their employment. A large percentage of clothes at cheap chain stores come from sweatshops, but clothes from more expensive stores and catalogs are not necessarily made without sweatshop labor.

- Cotton accounts for ten percent of worldwide pesticide use.

- Fur and fur trim come from wild animals that were either trapped or farmed. The most common trap, the steel jaw leghold trap, is excruciatingly painful. Unsuspecting animals step into the trap, and steel blades slam shut on their leg. The animals may then wait hours or sometimes days until the trapper comes to kill them. On fur farms, wild animals are confined in tiny, filthy cages where their natural instincts are thwarted. These animals are normally killed by gassing or anal electrocution.

- Leather usually comes from cows or pigs raised on factory farms. Tanneries, which turn the animals' skin into leather, use a variety of toxic chemicals that often pollute rivers.

✳

LET KINDNESS GROW

- Boycotts work! When consumers refuse to purchase products from a company whose policies are unethical or that produces materials which are environmentally hazardous, the company's profits decline. Well-publicized boycotts have had an enormous positive influence. For example, an international boycott of Nestlé led to the passage of the World Health Organization's International Code of Marketing for Breast Milk Substitutes. Nestlé had been providing infant formula free to new mothers in Africa. By using the formula, these mothers lost their own breast milk and were then compelled to buy formula they couldn't afford. When these mothers then diluted the formula with contaminated water, their children sometimes died. A successful boycott changed this practice.

- Your dollar is your vote. When you spend your money on products, you are essentially telling the company, "Do it again." Just as a boycott is a no vote, a *buy*cott is a yes vote.

- More and more companies are committed to producing clothes without using sweatshop labor. You will find information about assessing companies in the Helpful Hints section at the end of this book.

  By asking stores and companies about their policies when you purchase clothes, you will not only learn which companies do and don't employ sweatshop labor, you'll also be letting store owners and company executives know that you care about such issues, which in turn will influence their policies.

- Warm clothes don't have to come from factory-farmed animals. Eco-fleece, produced by companies such as Patagonia, is made from recycled plastics.

- Demand for organic cotton, like organic food, is on the rise which means prices are coming down and availability is increasing. Hemp clothing and footwear is an alternative to conventional cotton or leather. Visit <www.greenpages.org> to find out about companies that produce environmentally friendly clothes.

- Shopping at thrift shops not only saves money, it also reduces waste, decreases the use of production and distribution resources, and helps stem the tide of development for shopping malls and big box stores.

- A letter to your senator or representative about issues that concern you makes a difference. Often, legislators will establish a committee to look into an issue if they receive a mere ten letters on the subject.

TRYING TO LIVE WITH KINDNESS

When you first start analyzing your choices with the goal of modeling a humane life for your child, it can seem overwhelming. It's impossible to look at every choice we make, and we can wind up feeling immobilized, wondering what's best in each situation. When I first started down this path, I found it daunting. I knew what being kind meant in the context of my family and friends, and I had enough trouble being consistently kind to the people I loved most. How on earth could I be kind in all my choices? How could I make certain that by using certain products, by eating certain foods, by picking certain entertainments, I was kind to everyone whom my choices affected? How could I be that aware, let alone that disciplined? And how could I model for my son what it means to try to live humanely toward all?

Then I realized the answer. It was embedded in the very questions I was asking myself. I was going to *try*. I didn't have to live or model a perfectly humane life (assuming I even knew what a perfectly humane life looked like). What I could do, and what was no longer so daunting, was that I could *try* to live with kindness and respect for all. In so doing I would be modeling exactly what I wanted for my own child — that he try, too. And the way that I would try would be to use the Four Elements in a systematic and conscious way.

I had plenty of reverence to provide the fuel for the journey, but the Four Elements start with seeking information. How was I going to know what information I needed to live more humanely? I discovered that the key to actually using the Four Elements was simply to have an attitude of receptivity. All I needed to jumpstart the process was an inkling, the barest sense that something deserved my attention, and I was on my way. Then I could gather information, think about it, and turn new knowledge into respectful, responsible choices. Or at least I could try.

Trying to be the best person I can be, endeavoring to live according to my deepest values, staying open to discovering how I can be kinder and live with more integrity has given me more self-respect than I ever had before I started this journey. It's true that learning about how my choices affect others has also meant learning about suffering in the world. I have exposed myself to information that is painful, and I have felt both enormous rage and tremendous sorrow. Yet I am actually happier in general. This may seem counterintuitive, but I think the reason I'm more joyful now, despite having made myself more aware of suffering, is that I'm on a path that is meaningful and helpful. The information I've gathered has inspired me to make different choices, and those choices have been deeply satisfying because it feels good to live with more integrity. I like knowing that my choices can help improve the world. Even my relationships are more intimate and fulfilling because I'm open to learning how I can be a better parent, a better spouse, and a better friend.

ELAINE

My friend Elaine and I have known each other for fifteen years. We met when we were in our mid-twenties. She was working for a social justice organization where I had been a volunteer. Elaine knew about my work in humane education, but she never asked me questions. Almost a decade passed, and one day she said to me, "Zoe, I'm ready. I want to read everything you've got." I wasn't sure what she meant, so I asked her what she was ready for. "To learn about food," she replied. So I loaded her up with reading material, loaned her the award-winning video *Diet for a New America*, and gave her some cookbooks. She began to eat healthier and more humane foods, her asthma abated, and she lost weight.

When I reflect upon Elaine's process toward change, what strikes me is that she had to wait until she was ready to learn. She wasn't motivated by guilt to change her diet. Instead, there came a time when she was motivated by enthusiasm to create something better in her life.

For some it might be hard to imagine that what they're about to embark on when they use the Four Elements is an enriching, positive journey. It can often feel easier to shy away from information than to stay open to potentially life-changing choices. As a humane educator I have taught many courses that, among other things, unveil the hidden suffering and destruction in our world. Periodically, someone will tell me that they just don't want to know. What I think these people are really saying is this: "If you tell me this information, I will be faced with the choice of either changing or living without integrity, and I don't want to do either!" But, like my friend Elaine, choosing to learn, think, and act in concert with our values brings both joy and peace. That might sound trite, but it's true. Elaine felt better about herself. She was more vibrant and alive when she took a pro-active role in her life choices. She not only experienced the positive effects to her health, she also felt the positive effects to her soul when she made conscious and humane choices. If we all recognize that making and modeling humane choices actually increases our own joy, we will be as enthusiastic as Elaine.

As you consider your daily choices and make changes in your life to better reflect your values in relation to everyone and everything, you will begin to notice that the reverence, respect, and responsibility that you demonstrate will transform not only you, but also your whole family. You will likely discover that apathy and lack of interest are replaced with curiosity, commitment, desire for more shifts toward contentment with what you have and toward peacefulness. How is it possible that all this good can come from making kinder choices in relation to distant neighbors? It is possible because the great majority of the time when we act with kindness, the benefits rebound upon us tenfold. The kindest choices practically always turn out to be the healthiest, most sustaining, most enlivening, and ultimately most fulfilling ones.

DID YOU KNOW
THIS ABOUT MODERN AGRICULTURE?

- Conventional foods are usually produced using pesticides (fungicides, insecticides, and herbicides). These toxic chemicals do not remain confined to crops. They can seep into the ground destroying the delicate balance of healthy soil, pollute streams and rivers, and harm wildlife.

- Nonorganic coffee contributes to rainforest destruction, species extinction, and exposure of farmers to toxic chemicals.

- Some cocoa plantations, especially in certain African countries, employ slave labor.

- Animals concentrate pollutants and toxins in their flesh. When animals are fed nonorganic grain, their bodies become contaminated with pesticides. While people can wash apples to rinse off pesticide residues, they cannot wash their milk, eggs, or meat.

- Fish are especially likely to have high concentrations of toxins in their flesh. The EPA frequently issues warnings to women in their child-bearing years about consuming certain fish. Large fish eat smaller fish who eat smaller fish, which concentrates poisons such as PCBs and mercury up the food chain.

- Farmed fish are often diseased due to crowding in pens, and their huge quantities of waste can pollute nearby bays.

- The vast majority of meat comes from factory farms where animals suffer a range of mistreatment, including severe confinement, mutilation without anesthesia, and denial of their basic behavioral needs.

- Ninety-five percent of eggs come from hens confined in cages for their whole lives. Egg-laying facilities cram chickens together so tightly they are unable to move or stretch a wing. In order to prevent the dominant chickens from killing the rest of their cage mates in these conditions, all the chickens have half of their beaks cut off without anesthesia.

- Factory farming not only causes animals to suffer, it causes environmental problems as well. In one day in 1995, twenty-five million gallons of hog excrement spilled into a North Carolina river when the cesspool holding eight acres of pig waste burst. The spill's immediate consequence was to kill over ten million fish. Such spills are not uncommon.

- Dairy cows are normally impregnated annually, and their calves are usually taken away within 24 hours of birth. The milk meant for the calves is then collected for human consumption. Selective breeding and genetically engineered hormones injected into the cows have increased cows' milk production from seven pounds to over 70 pounds per day. This is the equivalent of cows having to nurse ten offspring instead of one. The result of this manipulation is frequent mastitis, a painful udder infection, and rampant use of antibiotics to combat it.

- Humans are the only mammal to drink milk beyond weaning and to drink the milk of another species. Most people in the world are unable to digest milk beyond childhood.

- Factory farms put small family farmers out of business. As agriculture is consolidated, family farmers are unable to compete with huge agribusiness corporations.

- Slaughterhouses used to kill about 50 cattle each hour. Twenty years ago the number rose to about 175. Today, some plants kill 400 cattle per hour.

Due to the sped-up slaughter lines, many animals are still alive when their throats are slit.

- According to the U.S. Bureau of Labor Statistics, meatpacking (slaughterhouse work) is the most dangerous job in the United States. Severe worker injuries — including lost limbs or fingers, debilitating repetitive motion syndromes, deep wounds, and back injuries — are commonplace and go largely unreported because employees worry that they will be fired if they speak out.

LET KINDNESS GROW

- Food co-ops, health food stores, and even some supermarkets have a large selection of organic, fair-trade (produced without slave labor), and nonfactory-farmed foods. While organic foods generally cost more than conventional foods, costs are coming down as more consumers make the choice to purchase humane and environmentally friendly foods.

- CSA (Community-Supported Agriculture) may be available in your community. These farm collectives enable you to support local organic farmers and to receive weekly produce in exchange.

- A complete vegetarian (vegan) diet reduces the risk of heart disease from almost 50 percent to about five percent, and is also associated with a reduced risk of certain cancers, stroke, hypertension, impotence, and kidney disease.

- With even a small backyard or deck, you can grow some of your own foods. Mel Bartholemew's *Square Foot Gardening* provides a wealth of information about how to grow your own vegetables and herbs in very little space.

- You'll find cookbook suggestions in the Resources to help you learn how to cook nutritious, tasty, and humane meals.

APPLYING THE FOUR ELEMENTS TO PERSONAL CHOICES

To use the Four Elements, you basically follow the same steps described in the previous chapter, except that instead of teaching your child, you will be evaluating your own personal choices. The following story about Maggie, a mother and homemaker living in coastal Maine, illustrates how someone can use the Four Elements as a tool for personal growth and humane choice-making.

MAGGIE

Maggie was watching a talk show about the trend toward genetically engineered (GE) crops. There were several guests on the program, including an environmentalist, a scientist, a nutritionist from the industry, and a representative from the company that produced the seeds. Maggie hadn't realized how many genetically engineered foods were on the shelves of the supermarket and how many of these foods she was already serving her two young children. She listened to the different perspectives, and when the show was over, she realized that she still didn't have enough knowledge to make a truly informed choice about what foods she would buy.

Maggie decided to get more information. She did an Internet search, and discovered a wealth of resources, both pro and con. She contacted several organizations and the companies who produce genetically engineered seeds, and asked questions. She didn't simply get one side of the story, but rather she gathered information from a range of sources and thought critically about everything she read and heard.

On the pro-genetic-engineering side, Maggie learned that GE crops promised to reduce pesticide use because the plants themselves would now be poisonous to various insects. There was also the potential for significantly increased crop yields, which could help alleviate world hunger concerns, and the possibility of increasing vitamin content in certain plants. On the flip side, she learned that certain crops were being genetically engineered to withstand herbicides so that farmers could spray even more chemicals to inhibit weeds without destroying the food crop itself, and that the majority of genetically engineered plants were feed crops for animals rather than grains meant to alleviate world hunger.

Maggie also learned that some genetically engineered crops could not be contained within specific farms because their seeds spread naturally into the ecosystem. This concerned her quite a bit. Even though she was not convinced that eating genetically engineered crops was dangerous to her family's health, she felt strongly that irreversibly introducing pesticide-resistant crops into the environment could have serious consequences as insects became resistant to the engineered plants. She was also concerned about the organic farmers whose crops were cross-pollinating with the GE plants, thus making them no longer organic. There were several organic farmers who lived near her, and she wondered what would happen if their fields were contaminated by neighboring GE crops.

Maggie saw a notice in the paper that a journalist would be speaking on the subject of genetic engineering at a local school one evening, and also found out that there was a group heading to Augusta, the state capitol, to speak to legislators about their concerns about genetically modified organisms (GMOs, synonymous with GE). She decided to get involved. She went to the talk and enjoyed listening to the speaker. He was smart and funny, and he, too, found the subject complex. He didn't entirely oppose genetic engineering, but nor did he support it except in limited circumstances. He was very concerned about the dangers of unrestricted genetic engineering and thought that our society and government should exercise extreme caution with this new technology.

Maggie decided to go with the group to visit her state legislators. While she wasn't an expert, she had done enough research to converse intelligently about the topic and raise important issues. She felt that her senator and representative really listened and that her visit had been quite worthwhile.

Back home Maggie decided she would try to avoid genetically engineered foods as much as possible. While she still wasn't sure whether these foods were hazardous to her family's health, she didn't want to support a technology that she believed was environmentally dangerous. She began reading labels to find the non-GMO stamp, and started buying organic food whenever she could. (For more information on GE foods, see the Helpful Hints section at the end of the book.)

Maggie didn't consciously set out to use the Four Elements, but nonetheless they were the tools she utilized. She became aware of an issue and then did some research (Element 1). She gathered information from a variety of sources, listened to different perspectives, and thought carefully about what she was learning (Element 2). She considered the effects on the environment and family farmers (relying upon her reverence), chose to err on the side of caution (showing respect), and took responsibility by meeting with her legislators to share her concerns and ask questions (Element 3). Lastly, she made some new choices based on her knowledge and values (Element 4).

DID YOU KNOW
THIS ABOUT AMERICAN CONSUMPTION?

The statistics in this box come from *All Consuming Passion: Waking Up from the American Dream* (3rd edition, 1998), where they are all referenced. See Helpful Hints section at the end of the book for more statistics from this publication.)

- Americans account for five percent of the world's population, yet consume approximately 30 percent of the world's resources, own 32 percent of the world's cars, and produce 22 percent of the world's climate-altering carbon dioxide.

- The amount of energy used by one American is equivalent to that used by
  > 3 Germans
  > 6 Mexicans
  > 14 Chinese
  > 38 Indians.

- It would require Four Earths for everyone on the planet to live the lifestyle of North Americans.

- The U.S. has lost
  > 50 percent of its wetlands
  > 85 percent of its old-growth forests
  > 99 percent of its tall-grass prairie
  > 520 species of native plants and animals
  > with 6,000 now being at risk

- 2,200 calories of energy are required to produce a 12-ounce can of diet soda, yet the soda only contains 1 calorie of food energy.

LET KINDNESS GROW

- According to Juliet Shor's *The Overspent American*, between 1990 and 1996 nearly 19 percent of adult Americans made a voluntary lifestyle change to improve their lives that entailed earning less money (not including regularly scheduled retirement). Nearly half of them made $35,000 or less before their change. Eighty-five percent of them report that they are happy about that change.

- By simplifying one's life, one gains more time, more money, and more peace of mind while having to deal with less clutter and less stress.

- With the advent of new technologies (from solar and wind energy to compact fluorescent light bulbs to hydrogen-powered fuel cells), consumers can now choose to significantly reduce their impact on the environment while largely maintaining their lifestyle.

- The choice to adopt or to have only one, or at most two, biological children has perhaps the greatest positive impact on the environment and other species by reducing resource use, pollution, and the growing danger of human overpopulation. Since, on average, each American uses as much energy as 38 Indians, human population growth is not solely a problem in other countries.

STEPS TO USING THE FOUR ELEMENTS

1. GATHER INFORMATION. In order to use the Four Elements yourself, consider the list of choices introduced above (under Expanding Humane Values to Include Everyone, page 57). Do you have a feeling that some of your choices in these different categories could be kinder? Are there areas where you sense that a little more information would help you make more compassionate decisions? Have you heard or seen anything that calls into question any particular choices? Has reading any of the "Did you know?" boxes made you aware of the effects of a choice that you hadn't thought about before? If your answer to any of these questions is "yes," then you already know some of what you need to learn. In addition to more information about the issues raised in the boxes, the Resources at the end of this book also offer reading suggestions, names of organizations, and web addresses. As you recognize areas where you could use more information, you'll probably be able to find a resource to help get you started.

2. THINK CRITICALLY. As you gather information, make sure to expose yourself to a variety of points of view in order to think critically and deeply. You can endeavor to obtain knowledge from reliable sources so that you are confident that your opinions are based on accurate and trustworthy information. Learning about different perspectives and struggling to sort through conflicting opinions will help you to become ever wiser.

3. USE THE THREE Rs. The three Rs can be the guiding principles in your process of choice-making. By nurturing your reverence, you will be ever more prepared to respect others and take responsibility for your choices. As you seriously consider the effects of your choices, you will find that your reverence (for loved ones, for yourself, for people worldwide, for the earth, and for other species) often inspires you to make more respectful and responsible decisions. Getting outdoors into nature, reading a biography about an inspiring historical figure, attending religious services,

gathering with people whose company supports and nourishes you, creating rituals around meaningful holidays or events, or even making a habit of spending a few minutes simply watching your sleeping children can all nurture your reverence and deepen your respect for and sense of responsibility towards all that you love. But you need not rely solely upon reverence to determine whether or not you will be respectful and responsible. You can also rely upon your commitment to values of justice and fairness to help you make the most respectful and responsible decisions.

4. MAKE POSITIVE CHOICES. After you have considered the information you've gathered and used the three Rs as your guide, you can ask yourself, "What choice will be kindest?" While none of us will always make the most humane choices, good decisions will flow naturally from the first three elements. Although we will inevitably fail to live up to our own deepest values all the time, the best way to consistently make kind choices is to stay mindful. Choosing to be humane means lifting up the veil of denial each time it falls between our most enduring wish to do good and our most eager efforts to avoid fear or struggle. It is when we are willing to look at the destruction we have caused and continue to cause that we can choose to restore and repair. Sometimes the competing impulses may be too strong to outweigh your desire to be more humane, but the more you pause and consider your choices, the more often you will choose the one that is ultimately the most kind. As your choices change, your life will become ever more the message you want it to be.

As you use the Four Elements, they will become incorporated into your life in a fluid and ordinary manner. You won't be doing homework each week or fretting over decisions. Rather, the Four Elements will simply become the way in which you go about questioning, learning, choosing, parenting — in short, living.

Most readers of this book will be in the privileged position to actually use these four elements to take on the challenges of living and modeling a humane life. Around the world, however, millions of parents are barely able to feed their children and survive. Many are victims of extreme deprivation and oppression. These parents cannot be charged with the task of dismantling inhumane systems of exploitation in which they themselves are victims. Those of us who can choose the products we use, the foods we eat, and the work we do are privileged beyond the wildest dreams of most of the world's population. Such privilege calls upon us to be ever more responsible about our choices.

DID YOU KNOW
THIS ABOUT THE EFFECTS OF
CONSUMER PRODUCTS?

- An SUV uses so much more fuel than a station wagon that choosing an SUV may be equivalent to leaving your refrigerator open for the duration of your refrigerator's life.

- Most paints, thinners, wood, rugs, and household cleaners contain toxic chemicals.

- Most personal care and household products (including cosmetics, soaps, shampoos, and cleaners) are routinely tested on unanesthetized animals. These products are forcefed to rodents to determine the quantity that is lethal, they are poured into the eyes of rabbits to determine eye irritancy, and they are smeared onto the shaved skin of animals to determine dermal toxicity.

✳

LET KINDNESS GROW

- Hybrid cars are twice as fuel-efficient as conventional sedans, and conventional station wagons are almost twice as fuel-efficient as SUVs.

- Nontoxic paints, rugs, strippers, wood, and sealants are available from some stores and through mail-order catalogs. See the Helpful Hints section at the end of the book for information on obtaining environmentally friendly household products.

- Danny Seo's *Conscious Style Home* offers useful tips for building or redecorating with environmentally friendly, nontoxic materials.

- Hundreds of companies do not test their products on animals and instead use non-animal methods for assuring safety. You'll find a list of these "cruelty-free" companies in the Helpful Hints. Additionally, you can look for the non-animal-tested bunny logo on personal care products.

A WANT OR A NEED?

One of the best ways to assess our choices is to ask ourselves this: "Is what I am about to do or buy a want or a need?" It's remarkable how many things we call "needs." All we and our children really *need* is healthy food, clean water, clean air, fertile soil, shelter and protective clothing, education for basic knowledge and a skill or craft, and kind and loving relationships. Yet who among us feels that everything else is but a desire when our culture so adamantly proclaims that we need so much more. We can barely disentangle true needs from desires.

Here's a simple example of a want that is perceived as a need: Only a small percentage of Americans would probably agree that we don't actually *need* commercial cleaners, yet our grandparents knew that baking soda and white vinegar could be used for the majority of household cleaning jobs. Choosing these two edible products would result in:

- lower costs for cleaning products
- no danger of accidental poisoning of our children
- less animal testing
- less waste of resources
- less pollution
- no chemical odor when we clean
- no allergic reactions to toxic chemicals

Why don't more of us use baking soda and vinegar to clean our homes? Because we've been taught through advertising to buy products that we don't need (and that are usually poisonous, cruelly tested on animals, and costly). Corporations have created in us a need that does not really exist. True, there are times when certain manufactured cleaners do a better job than baking soda and vinegar, but homemade cleaners are sufficient for the majority of tasks.

Advertising works to convince us that our deepest needs will be met with things, and over time we've begun to conflate the things themselves with our basic needs. Many of us have come to believe that a new lipstick or cologne, a new brand of jeans or depilatory, a weight loss program or hair dye will make us happier. "In order to be one with everything, you must have one of everything" reads the copy on an advertisement for a Ford truck, with the photo of a smiling young man in the lotus position surrounded by material objects offering quite a cynical view of the world. The ad may be tongue-in-cheek, but it plays on our deepest spiritual yearnings and suggests that we can fulfill our quest for nirvana by purchasing a Ford pick-up.

Most of us think we're unaffected by advertising. Ask the average person if advertising influences her buying habits, and you'll usually be told no. I used to argue vehemently that advertising had no effect on me. Although I grew up watching a lot of television, I thought I was too smart to fall for advertising messages. Years later I realized how much I'd actually been influenced by all those early years of TV. My in-laws were coming over for dinner, and I had taken down our rarely used wine glasses from the cupboard. I noticed there were water spots on them. I paused. How many times had I laughed at the Cascade commercials featuring actors who bemoaned spots on glasses and thought to myself, "How can anyone really think that people care about water spots on glasses? Who are they kidding!?" Confronted with spots on my glasses, and my in-laws about to arrive, I furiously started cleaning the glasses. I even thought, "I wonder if Cascade really prevents such problems?" (I had quickly decided that spots on glasses were, indeed, a problem.) I never did buy Cascade, choosing instead a dish soap which came from a company that did not conduct animal tests and which was more environmentally friendly, but I finally admitted that I had indeed been affected by advertising.

Most of us can find examples of advertising messages creeping into our consciousness unwelcome and unanalyzed. And most of us want to conform to social norms, at least to some extent. And so thousands of products become, over time, needs. But if we become aware of the true costs of our choices, it is possible for a need to become a recognizable want — and perhaps eventually a "don't want" — because we don't want to contribute to suffering. There's nothing wrong with satisfying our desires along with our needs as long as we are able to distinguish between the two and make humane choices about what we do and what we buy. By bringing to awareness the fact that we are always making choices for ourselves and our children and by committing to make those choices ever more humane, we will be able to satisfy our true needs without hurting others in the process.

Advertising not only influences our buying habits, it often makes us feel insecure. I worried that my in-laws would think their son married a severely cleanliness-challenged woman if I didn't live up to the standard created by Cascade commercials. How many children feel bad because they don't have the newest toy or the cereal with the prize in it that's advertised on TV? How many families have gone into debt to live up to a standard created by advertising? It is virtually impossible to remain immune to commercial messages that promote both insecurity and the acquisition of material goods.

AVOIDING RATIONALIZATIONS

Being willing to learn and change requires that we be gentle with ourselves as we try to make kinder choices, yet it is also important to guard against rationalizations. It is all too easy to choose the less humane product and to rationalize the decision with internal comments like "My choosing this won't really make a difference." Better to be honest with ourselves, to truly recognize that we are consciously making a decision that may be causing harm, and to understand our deeper motives and competing desires that led to that decision. Rationalizations perpetuate superficial thinking and impede good judgment, and they teach our children to abandon their empathy, honesty, and intellect in favor of deception. Unless we grapple with the qualities within us that allow us to disregard others, we will, in our own ways, perpetuate suffering.

But here is the good news. The more we divest ourselves of manufactured needs and desires, the happier and more peaceful we actually become. It's exhausting to want and pursue "things," far more exhausting in fact than being attentive to the true costs of our choices. As we free ourselves from attachments to material possessions, we also free ourselves to enjoy the true pleasures of life: relationships, real leisure, contemplation, hobbies, and often more fulfilling work.

DID YOU KNOW
THIS ABOUT ADVERTISING'S
INFLUENCE ON CHILDREN?

- Advertisers have coined the phrase "cradle to grave" marketing to refer to their efforts to create brand loyalties from the time a child is old enough to recognize jingles or company logos.

- About $1 billion is spent on toy advertising annually.

- According to industry studies, a person's "brand loyalty" may begin as early as age two.

- According to the Annenberg Public Policy Center, the average American child (aged 2 to 17) watches seventeen and a half hours of TV each week, viewing over 20,000 TV commercials per year.

- The American Academy of Pediatrics reports that the average American child (aged 2-18) "spends nearly five and a half hours a day out of school consuming media in the form of TV, music, magazines, video games and the internet."

- Channel One, a 12-minute news and advertising TV program, is viewed daily in 12,000 middle and high schools across America during 90 percent of the school days. The program is a for-profit commercial enterprise to sell advertising spots to companies. Soft drinks, candy, and high fat, processed foods are frequently advertised to students who are required to watch the program at school.

- According to a Junior Achievement poll, 43 percent of teenagers associate the American Dream with the accumulation of material possessions.

LET KINDNESS GROW

The Center for a New American Dream (from which many of the statistics above were compiled) held an art and essay contest asking children, age five to 17, "What do you really want that money can't buy?" Below are some responses:

"Money could never buy the conversations that my Dad and I have in the car on the way to hockey practice. We talk about everything that you could think of. We talk about friends and about what is going on in the world ... I love the time with my Dad and no one or no thing could replace it."

— Seth, age 11

"I want to play in the snow every winter. I want to swim in the ocean every summer. I want to plant trees in the park with my friends every spring. I want to jump in puddles every autumn. I want to adopt a homeless dog and a little kitten from a shelter (Mom, please let me!) and teach them never to fight. I want there to be peace on Earth and I want people to take better care of our planet."

— Anastasia, age 10

"I want peace; a quietness for my soul. And ease for my thoughts and a rest for my heart ... I want faith. To possess the substance of things hoped for and the evidence of things not seen ..."

— Elisa, age 14

The voices of these children remind us about what is truly important. The more we parents turn off the TV and play with our children, or take them on family and community outings, the less we expose ourselves and them to commercial values that will shape their desires and behaviors in ways that do not really serve them or the world. By limiting or eliminating commercial television in our households and teaching our children to view commercial messages critically, we help them identify and strive for the fulfillment of their deepest dreams.

CONFRONTING THE OBSTACLES

About now, the boxes in this chapter may have you thinking, "I can't worry about all these issues and concerns. My life is too busy. I don't have time to find humanely produced clothes and products. I can't afford to buy organic foods. And what would we do without television? Maybe I can be kinder and more compassionate to my kids, but I can't do much more!" Before putting this book down and deciding that it's too much work to make humane choices on behalf of everyone, take a deep breath and remind yourself about what you really care about. If the first thing that comes to mind is "My kids," then remember that all these possibilities for modeling a humane message are *for* your kids. The choices you make today will influence the choices they make as they grow up. Choosing to make humane choices will not only help your children now, it will also help create a better world in which they can achieve their potential.

PRACTICAL TIPS FOR MODELING YOUR MESSAGE

Here are some concrete ways to tackle competing impulses and to better model your message:

- Find or create a practice that helps you to deeply connect with your true self, your soul, your deepest beliefs. This might happen through meditation, prayer, time in nature, conscious physical exercise (such as Yoga or Tai Chi), or journal writing. Commit to a practice every day, even if it is only a few minutes.

- Before you go to sleep each night, take stock of your day. Observe in your mind's eye the choices you made. Ask yourself: "What did I learn? For what am I grateful? What could I have done better?"

- Make the words "My life is my message" a mantra.

- With your spouse, a friend, or a group of parents share your progress toward living more humanely. Commit to meeting once a week to once a month to support each other in your efforts.

- Acknowledge your feelings! If you find yourself wanting to toss your recyclables in the trash, stop at McDonald's rather than fix a nutritious meal for your family, buy a product tested on animals, not give more to a worthy charity drive — whatever the impulse or desire — ask yourself: "What is my underlying feeling?" You may have to ask yourself this a few times to uncover the deepest level of truth. Let yourself really feel whatever emotions make you want to make choices that are not in the best interests of you, your children, or the world. Give the feeling voice; let it be heard in your heart and mind and soul. Then ...

- Ask yourself what you really want, what you really yearn for, what is really important to you.

- Breathe deeply and weigh the competing emotions. Make a conscious decision about your choices. Don't permit yourself to rationalize. Acknowledge your feelings in response to your decisions, be they decisions stemming from desires or fears or from kindness and compassion.

- Judge without being judgmental. Be gentle and compassionate with yourself. Your kindness toward and acceptance of yourself despite all your imperfections will, almost para-doxically, allow you to make more humane choices.

DID YOU KNOW
THIS ABOUT COMPANION ANIMALS?

- Millions of dogs and cats are killed in shelters and SPCAs every year for lack of homes.

- Wild birds are still captured for the pet trade. Only about half of the birds who are caught make it to pet stores alive.

- Many purebred dogs and cats come from puppy mills where their mothers are mistreated and forced to deliver litter after litter in cramped and unsanitary conditions.

- Dogs and cats are sometimes stolen and sold to biological supply companies (to become dissection specimens) or to testing laboratories.

- Cats are non-indigenous predators, and millions of songbirds are killed annually by cats who are permitted to roam outside.

LET KINDNESS GROW

- In general, mixed breed animals have fewer health problems than purebreds.

- When people spay and neuter their companion animals and adopt animals from shelters and SPCAs, they reduce the numbers of healthy dogs and cats who are killed for lack of homes.

- For those people who really want a certain breed of dog or cat, a visit to the Internet can steer them toward rescue organizations for specific breeds.

- Cats are less likely to be lost, get in fights, contract diseases, or be hit by cars if they're kept indoors. In general, indoor cats live much longer than cats who go outside.

- Visits to wildlife sanctuaries and rehabilitation centers allow our children to see and learn about wild animals without harming them.

FINANCIAL OBSTACLES

Obstacles on the journey toward compassionate living are not always internal. One of the obstacles that many people face is financial. Humane choices can sometimes be more costly than mainstream choices. For example, organic food and clothing are generally more expensive because our government subsidizes conventional produce, meat, dairy, and eggs, and there are fewer farmers who grow sustainable, organic crops. Yet, despite the higher costs of organics, even people with few financial resources who want to live according to humane values can find ways to make humane food and clothing choices.

My friend Heather has experienced financial hardship her whole life, but her choices have been very ecologically sound, largely because she has had to learn ways to conserve resources.

Unable to afford a clothes dryer, for example, she hung her laundry on a clothesline. Because new clothes were often too expensive for their family budget, she usually shopped at thrift stores. To keep food costs down, she became part of a cooperative buying club that purchased cases of groceries at low cost and then divided the food between the members of the group. The buying co-op was associated with an organic foods distributor, so the majority of her groceries were organic. When Heather came to a compassionate living workshop at our Institute several years ago, she realized that she'd been making environmentally friendly choices by necessity. While others in the group were learning how they might conserve energy and resources, Heather discovered she'd been doing this all along.

I do not want to suggest that every family has the means to make the most humane choices in all situations, but often financial concerns can be met when we deeply evaluate our priorities and commitments. The fact that people with severe economic restraints have found ways to live deeply humane lives suggests that money isn't usually the primary obstacle. Lack of discipline and commitment are often bigger hurdles to overcome.

Nonetheless, if you are reading this book and your economic situation is grim, and your options seem extremely limited, there are ways to tackle them. The following suggestions are not only money-saving, they are also humane:

- Buy whole grains, cereals, and beans in bulk at food co-ops or neighborhood buying clubs (like Heather does), and divvy them up with friends. You'd be amazed at how inexpensive healthy, organic food can be if purchased this way.
- Set up a clothing swap with friends and neighbors and hand down your outgrown clothes while collecting clothes for your kids. The same can be done with outgrown athletic equipment including cleats, shin guards, knee pads, ice skates, skis, baseball gloves, and toys.
- Go to yard sales, libraries, and secondhand stores first

before heading to the chain stores.

- Share what you have. Do you have tools that your neighbor could use? Does your neighbor have a tiller that you could borrow to create a garden plot? There are so many things that we use infrequently, and with a commitment to sharing we could buy less and borrow and lend more.
- Find opportunities to barter. Do you have a skill to share? Can you offer babysitting to a neighbor in exchange for carpentry or car repair that you need?
- Head to the library and pick up *Your Money or Your Life* by Joe Dominguez and Vicki Robin. This book is so helpful when it comes to really assessing your monetary needs and expenditures and taking control over your economic situation.
- Once again, turn off the television. Chances are TV will make you want more while instilling in you a feeling of inadequacy because of what you cannot afford. Have your children's friends over and invite their parents so that you'll have company, too. Building community and partaking of simple pleasures will enable you to feel abundance rather than lack.

If you choose to reorient your lifestyle away from consumption of products, your financial needs will actually diminish. How many families are slaves to their work because they have become slaves to the marketplace? A growing movement of voluntary simplicity demonstrates that a pleasurable and meaningful life can be lived with less money than most people imagine, and many are giving up the hours in the office to have more hours at home, voluntarily reducing their monetary income so as to increase their simplicity income.

※

DO YOU KNOW WHICH HARMS LESS?

If you were to rate leisure activities on a scale of 1-10 (1 being least destructive to the environment, other species, and other people, and 10 being most destructive and energy-consumptive), how would you rate the following?

- Downhill skiing ___
- Cross-country skiing ___
- Cruise in the Caribbean ___
- Sailing trip ___
- ATV outings in the natural areas ___
- Climbing a mountain ___
- Water skiing ___
- Kayaking ___
- Snowmobiling ___
- Snowshoeing ___
- Indoor ice skating ___
- Outdoor ice skating ___
- Sport hunting ___
- Photographing wildlife ___
- Recreational fishing ___
- Canoeing ___
- Swimming in a pool ___
- Swimming in a lake or pond ___
- Playing golf (on a pesticide-covered course) ___
- Playing badminton (in your backyard) ___
- Attending a rodeo ___
- Attending a show of human acrobats ___

It's pretty clear from reading this list that some leisure activities come at a greater cost than others, and usually there is something similar, pleasurable (and often healthier) that we can do with our children that causes less harm and results in greater good.

MODELING HUMANE VALUES IN AN INHUMANE WORLD

It would be challenging enough to raise humane children in a humane culture, but when our culture sometimes teaches and reflects values we may distrust or even deplore, we are facing a much greater challenge. We are surrounded by messages that promote values which not only lead us away from truly humane living, but which actually endorse inhumane choices. However much we may try to shield our children and to model a different message, their peers and their culture will sometimes model values and beliefs that are in conflict with our own.

While the bad news is that you are not the sole influence on your children and that aspects of our culture may be working against you in your efforts to raise a humane child, the good news is that you have more power than you may realize. You can be part of a movement that will transform the culture around your children. You can build a community to create support for humane values. When you build such a community, you diminish the obstacles in your child's path. Eventually, our culture will not present us with so many obstacles to overcome, but rather will be an ally that mirrors our transformed world. Right now, however, you are a harbinger of that humane world, and your children need you to find and create for them a community whose life is a message of humane values. Here are some steps you can take to ensure that your children have such a community:

BECOME INVOLVED WITH WHAT IS ALREADY AVAILABLE

- Join your local food co-op. There you can find not only healthy and humane foods for your family, but also community. Food co-ops rely upon member volunteerism to keep costs lower and to run the cooperative, and this volunteerism builds community. Co-ops also have bulletin boards that list local resources for everything from parenting and playgroups to La Leche League meetings (to provide support for breastfeeding), to local community events, to alternative health care, to festivals and community entertainment. If you don't have a local food co-op, chances are that you have a natural foods grocery nearby that can offer many of the same benefits.

- Does your community have an alternative monetary exchange? If so, consider becoming part of it. Many communities around the country have created barter systems in which members of the community trade services rather than dollars. In Ithaca, NY, for example, an "Ithaca Hour" can be traded for a service. If you're a landscaper, you can offer your services for a certain amount of "Ithaca Hours." You might redeem these hours for piano lessons for your son. Such nonmonetary exchanges build a tremendous feeling of community as people meet one another and share talents and skills.

- Does your town or city have places of worship that speak to your spiritual needs and preach a commitment toward world stewardship? If so, visit them and find a spiritual community that supports your values. More and more churches, synagogues, mosques, and Buddhist temples are embracing the ethic of care that our world so desperately needs. Even very traditional institutions are recognizing that God does not want humans to despoil and destroy the Earth. Some fundamentalist churches around the country are speaking out against overconsumption as being anathema to God's will. For those people to whom institutionalized religion is unappealing, there are many congregations that welcome believers and atheists alike, preferring the creation of community built on the shared values of peace, justice, and compassion to those built around dogma.

- Are there nonprofit organizations in your community doing work that you support and that put your values into action? Join them! Volunteering with your family not only helps improve the world and fosters compassion and kindness, it also creates community.

CREATE WHAT YOU DON'T FIND

- Do you wish that your community had a food co-op? Start one! With a few families you can initiate a buying club (similar to Heather's) and get significant discounts on healthy, organic foods while building community at the same time. Our local food co-op began this way. When it became too big to remain a buying club, the members created a store and opened it to the public. When they outgrew their small space, they enlarged it and opened a cafe that serves primarily organic, whole foods. The walls of the cafe are decorated with the artwork of member artists, including children's art, and the co-op has become a gathering place for the extended community.
- Do you wish that your community had an alternative barter exchange? Contact the community organizers who established such exchanges in other towns and cities and create such an exchange yourself. Thomas Greco's *Money: Understanding and Creating Alternatives to Legal Tender* can help get you started.
- Do you wish you had other parents with whom to share ideas, thoughts, concerns, and conversation? Post a notice on the school or co-op bulletin board that invites people to join a parenting group. Then share books and articles and choose topics for discussion that will help you all become more humane parents and raise more humane children.
- Start a play group for your young children. Perhaps you'll want to create a group where there are no toy weapons, where healthy, organic snacks are offered to the children, where the parents and children make crafts together, and where singing, storytelling, and other circle activities are

part of each gathering. Such groups can sometimes lead to the formation of alternative schools if there are a few parents who are willing to take the lead and commit to creating a different learning environment for their children as they grow up.

- If someone in your neighborhood becomes ill, is injured, or needs help in some way, organize community efforts on their behalf. Plan for meals to be delivered, dogs walked, and the house tidied or cleaned. Such generosity not only helps your neighbor, it builds community. It may feel like a stretch to reach beyond the safe walls of home to meet the neighbors, but when you take such steps, you build support for your own family, too. True, reaching out to your neighbor does not ensure that you'll find a community that is deeply committed to living according to humane values in all their lifestyle choices, but it is a start. As you meet your neighbors, you can share your journey toward living a more humane life with them. You may find that others want to go on the journey, too.

- If none of the religious institutions in your area appeals to you, create your own group of seekers and celebrants. Perhaps you'll gather weekly to sing and dance and celebrate the beloved planet. Perhaps you'll meet for prayer vigils. Perhaps you'll come together to explore what living according to humane values means. Perhaps you'll celebrate the seasonal changes, the solstices and equinoxes. Perhaps you'll form circles of people to share your deepest selves. Whatever your calling, you can create a community that shares it.

This chapter has called upon you to assess your life and perhaps to change aspects of your lifestyle. It is my hope that reading it has felt like an opportunity to make better choices for yourself, your children, and the world. Remember to be compassionate towards yourself as you make new choices. Being open to learn and change, however slowly, is the biggest step you can take toward modeling your message.

To help you in the process of more fully embodying your values, I've included the "My Life Is My Message" Questionnaire on page 207. This questionnaire offers you the opportunity to reflect upon your life and to put into words some concrete goals for modeling your message. You may want to turn to it now.

FOUR

THE EARLY YEARS
(BIRTH THROUGH AGE 6)

If I had influence with the good fairy who is supposed to preside over the christening of all
children I should ask that her gift to each child
in the world be a sense of wonder so indestruc-
tible that it would last throughout life, as an
unfailing antidote against the sterile preoccupa-
tion with things that are artificial, the alienation
from the sources of our strength. If a child is to
keep alive his inborn sense of wonder without
any such gift from the fairies, he needs the com-
panionship of at least one adult who can share it,
rediscovering with him the joy, excitement and
mystery of the world we live in.

— RACHEL CARSON

DURING THEIR EARLY YEARS, children are soaking up every-thing around them. Long before they are able to articulate their feelings in words, they come to have fundamental beliefs based on their life experiences, and these beliefs in turn influence their attitudes and actions. In other words, it is during the early years that the foundation is laid for much of our children's later behaviors. If the foundation is strong, our children will likely be able to withstand storms and winds throughout their lives and remain true to themselves and their deepest beliefs.

This is the period in which many basic habits are formed. The norms you create in your home will provide the standard to which your children will return for many years to come. If you want to raise a humane child, the early years are the time to make sure that the standard you are creating is one that is compassion-ate towards and healthy for both your child and the world.

Young children learn primarily by imitating those around them: their parents, siblings, day-care providers, grandparents, neighbors — and the television and film characters to whom they are exposed. While they come into the world with their own per-sonalities, temperaments, and talents, young children learn the basics of what is right and wrong, how to behave or not behave, and which values are honored and which are eschewed by who and what they are exposed to. To foster those qualities you most want your children to embody, you must give them role models to emulate — and their primary role model is you, their parent.

Does your young child see you being generous? Compassionate? Honest? Courageous? Kind? Does she have rel-atives, nannies, or day-care providers who are people of character who model these qualities, too? When you are with your child, are you patient? Slow to anger and quick to forgive? Sympathetic? Clear and consistent? Self-disciplined? Able to judge without being judgmental? Fun and funny? Nurturing and loving? Are you actively working to make your life your message?

Reading these questions, especially after finishing Chapter 3, may feel exhausting. Writing them, I'm well aware that I don't consistently model all of these virtues or behaviors myself. I wish that I modeled them more often with Forest, and that I were not so impatient and quick-tempered. Humane qualities may be our goal, but we know better than to expect that any parent manages to model them all the time. Yet having the goal is critical. Every time we catch ourselves being short-tempered, inconsistent, or confusing, we can pause long enough to choose how to act, rather than simply react.

We teach our children how to cope with their own anger and frustration, their own feelings of rage and violence, their own tendencies toward greed and hoarding, their own emotions of jealousy and envy by how we cope with these feelings ourselves and by how well *we* are able to acknowledge our emotions while still choosing to act from our deepest wisdom and compassion.

Although this is a book about raising a humane child rather than raising a child humanely, the two go hand in hand, especially during the early years when who you are as a person and as a parent is what you are teaching your child to become. Even as I write these words, I find them so humbling as to make me want to run from this project and find a saint to write this book instead of me. Ironically, however, most saints are not parents. Some of the people I admire most, spiritual leaders like the Dalai Lama, do not have children. Others, like Mahatma Gandhi, perhaps the greatest teacher of nonviolence ever to have lived, have admitted that they were not always good parents. It is often easier to be our best with strangers than with our most beloved children. Yet if we truly want what is best for them, it will help to bring out the best in us.

Knowing that your own ability to embody the best qualities is the biggest teacher doesn't mean that there is nothing more that you can do to lay the foundation for raising a humane child during the early years. As we have seen, values and beliefs do not come solely from us parents. The wider culture reaches into our home with countless messages that may or may not reflect our own. The parents of a young child must choose how much of that wider culture to invite into the construction of their child's foundation. During the early years, parents can work to create a humane and healthy environment for their children knowing that the decisions they make may have long-lasting effects.

THE FOUR ELEMENTS DURING THE EARLY YEARS

In terms of the Four Elements described in Chapter 2, the early years of life are *not* the time to provide information about the ills of the world, the suffering of its people and animals, or the rapid destruction of the biosphere. Nor is it a time to cultivate deep critical thinking skills that will become so important later in life. As for providing choices, parents of infants and young children make the important decisions and offer their children only simple choices that fall within the comfort level and values of the parents themselves. Three of the Four Elements are basically irrelevant to the baby, toddler, and preschooler. But one of them is crucial: *helping your child to experience the first of the three Rs — Reverence.* Reverence is a critical part of the foundation that will support all the qualities mentioned in this book. As you nurture reverence in your young children, you not only give them the opportunity to have one of the most nourishing experiences that humans are capable of, you also inspire them to actively seek out and pursue the good throughout their lives.

One of the best places to start is nurturing reverence for the natural world. For the young child, nature offers food for the soul. Most American children spend more time in places like malls, grocery stores, and shopping centers than they do in the woods, at the ocean, running through meadows, swimming in lakes and rivers, smelling flowers, or even playing in the grass. Whether our babies are born in the deep of a northern winter or the heat of a southern summer, we can bring them outside to meet and fall in love with their true home. In so doing, we will be nurturing reverence and helping to ensure that when they grow up they will honor and protect their home, the earth.

As I mentioned earlier, I grew up in Manhattan, a place with little nature. But we lived near Central Park, and my mother would frequently take me to a playground there. While I enjoyed the sandbox and jungle gym, the slides and seesaws, my very favorite spot was a hill of rocks protruding from the grass about a hundred yards past the playground. I would play imaginary games and enact stories on these rocks for hours. Years later I visited the rocks and discovered that they were not the huge boulders that I'd experienced as a child. In fact, the whole area occupied a mere 300 square feet, and no rock was higher than my waist!

Don't we all have stories like this? Places in nature that ignited our imaginations and fed our souls with mystery and pleasure? Do our own children have such places? Are we taking our toddlers to indoor gym classes or malls more often than we take them outside to meet and interact with the mystery of the natural world? Are we giving our young children the opportunity to pick up and examine an oak leaf, to sink their small fingers into mud, to find an earthworm and marvel at him? Are we letting them play with acorns before we buy them countless plastic balls? When a friend of mine read these questions, she turned to me and said, "Let me tell you about my friend Sheila and Gymboree."

SHEILA AND LUCY

Sheila's daughter Lucy was only eighteen months old when Karen, a friend of Sheila's, told her she should sign Lucy up for Gymboree, an exercise and sensory class for infants and toddlers. Karen explained that it was important for Sheila to socialize Lucy and to give her opportunities to improve her coordination and balance. Not wanting Lucy to be deprived of the latest trend in toddler education, Sheila signed up for a class and brought Lucy to the indoor space where it was held.

Sheila was instructed to lie down on the mats and move Lucy's legs to the music. Next, she was told to do other exercises with some plastic props. Meanwhile, the sun was shining outside, and Lucy kept walking over to the glass doors to look out. Sheila took Lucy to a few more classes, but it always seemed as if she had to drag Lucy away from the yard in order to get to the class on time. Sheila began to think that Lucy would be better served by playing in the grass and dirt than going to toddler gym class.

When Sheila told Karen how she was feeling, Karen discouraged her from abandoning the class and asked her if she really wanted Lucy outside so much. Karen even mentioned that it might not be healthy for Lucy to be playing in the dirt because it was, "well, *dirty*." But Sheila didn't think it was actually healthier for Lucy to be playing indoors on the germ-covered mats with a dozen other toddlers, and she decided to trust her instincts and give Lucy the freedom to use her body in the fresh air and sunshine and to explore the world of nature in their small yard. She realized that she had been giving Lucy just what she needed after all.

THE CONSEQUENCES OF A LACK OF REVERENCE

When I was a teenager, my mother periodically told me that I didn't understand the real world. By this she meant the world of commerce and money-making, filled with people competing to succeed in that world. She told me this not to be negative or to make me become disillusioned, but out of concern for my welfare. She wanted to make sure that I knew how to succeed and cope in the real world. I have come to believe that few of us understand the real world, but I define it differently. It does not simply comprise our created world of technology and trade or our human-centered activities. The *real* world is the world of the water cycle, the seasons, the delicate balance of chemicals in the air, the ecology of the soil, the interplay of species, the journey of the spinning earth around the sun. This extraordinary, complex, and mysterious ball of life in an extraordinary, complex, and mysterious universe is the *real* world. If we confuse our human-centered world with ultimate reality, we not only shut our children off from the deepest understanding of themselves, from their sense of wonder, and from their potential connection to the source of all this magic and mystery, we also set them up to disregard the world that matters most of all. Without reverence and appreciation for this real world, commerce, technology, politics, economics, "success," and even basic human interactions may ultimately not be possible because we may fail to prevent the destruction of this very real, very precious world. When we reverently introduce our children to nature, we are introducing them to the real world and inspiring them to care for it.

In his book *Earth in Mind*, ecologist David Orr suggests that biophobia, a fear of nature, is not simply an inconvenient character trait. Biophobia leads relentlessly to environmental destruction. Our culture wants so desperately to control the nature we fear and to shape it to suit our aesthetic and emotional desires that we turn our backyards into sterile, lifeless carpets; turn our forests into monoculture feed crops and feedlots; and turn our fruits into waxed pyramids of red, yellow, or green in our supermarkets. We imprison lions, bears, and elephants and make them perform for us in circuses. We inflame bulls with painful straps cinched around their bellies and genitals and sharp spurs kicked into their bodies in order to demonstrate our power over them in rodeos, and choke terrified calves with ropes to subdue them. Over and over we offer these ways of interacting with animals and the natural world to our children, promoting domination and harm instead of nurturing reverence.

For decades, the small town of Hegins, Pennsylvania, held an annual Labor Day pigeon shoot. Many thousands of pigeons were captured and bred for the event, and caged until Labor Day arrived. The birds were placed in tiny boxes on a field where shooters lined up for the chance to kill the birds as the box doors were opened, and the dazed animals tried to fly away. Five thousand

birds were killed annually in just a few hours. One year I attended the shoot as a protester. A woman I knew there witnessed the
following interaction between a father and his son: The young
boy, naturally inclined to feel reverence, started to cry when he
saw what was happening to the birds. He turned his back to the
shooting field and held his father's pants, burying his head
against his father's body. His father did not comfort him. Instead,
he grabbed him by the shoulders, jerked him around to face the
field and told him to watch. The boy began to cry harder and
turned his back again, but this time his father swung him around,
held him in place, and said, "You *will* watch!"

Hegins no longer holds an annual slaughter of pigeons. The
Pennsylvania legislature has made such shoots illegal, but I have
often thought about the young boy whose compassion was pun-
ished. Presumably, he is a teenager now. Are his heart and soul
intact? Does he allow himself to love, to care, to empathize, and
to be vulnerable, or was his kind spirit and reverence for animals
crushed that day on the shooting field?

NURTURING REVERENCE

Instead of diminishing our children's love and compassion for
animals and the earth, we can widen and celebrate these feelings.
Rather than take our young children to circuses, we can take
them to nature preserves, wildlife sanctuaries, and rehabilitation
centers, to "zoos" for rescued animals rather than to zoos where
animals are bought, sold, and bred. Instead of taking our children to rodeos, we can allow them to experience the natural
world without the shadow of human cruelty. Rather than spray
our lawn with poisonous chemicals to kill unwanted plants, we
can let our lawn be imperfect-looking but safe. Our children
can even gather the dandelion "weeds," turn the flowers into
crowns to wear around their heads, and use the new dandelion
greens in salads. (New shoots of dandelion greens are very
nutritious and flavorful.) We can invite our children to explore

their own biophilia, their love of life, rather than cultivate a generation that is even more biophobic than our own.

My husband often wears a small magnifying glass attached to a string around his neck. We spend a great deal of time hiking and exploring in nature, and he will often stop to pull out the magnifying glass to observe ever more closely a leaf, a crystal, or a flower. When Forest was one year old, we spent a week on an island in the Gulf of Maine where we were the only people. One image in particular stands out in my mind when I think of that trip: my husband crouched down on the ground, his magnifying glass held close to the grass, with Forest peering down next to him. Forest was watching his dad watch the insects hidden in the grass. He was learning to revere what his father revered.

Any of us can carry a magnifying glass outdoors and offer it to our children to see the wonders of nature. When we hold that magnifying glass up to a spider web covered in morning dew or observe an ant carrying more than his own body weight on a journey that would put us to shame if we had to do comparable work or delve into the depths of a flower and notice the mysteries within, we nurture reverence in our children.

When we revere the magnificent earth and its creatures, the earth reveals itself ever more to our senses and to our hearts and souls. Our children's spirits will soar when they watch the vermilion sun sink below a pink sky as it sets in the west. They will marvel at the speed and agility of a bat hunting for insects at dusk, and their own eyes will light up, as if in reflection, when they witness the light of a thousand fireflies at twilight. Like Lucy, they will be delighted just to play in the dirt and grass in their backyard or nearby park.

THE WONDER WALK

The Wonder Walk is my very favorite activity for nurturing reverence. You can do it with your children once they are about three or four years old and continue doing it throughout their childhood.

Choose a spot outdoors, preferably a quiet backyard, park, woodland, or meadow, and hold your child's hand. Explain that you will be taking him on a very special journey. Tell him that he will have his eyes closed most of the time and that the whole activity is done in silence. Let him know that when you tap next to his eyes, he should open them; when you touch the tip of his nose, he should smell deeply; when you put his hands on something, or place something in his hands, he is being invited to touch; when you tap his earlobe, it is his signal to listen; and when you touch his lips, he should part them to receive something to eat. Remind him that after each experience, he should close his eyes again.

Carefully begin leading your child on his Wonder Walk, looking around to discover what it is you want to show him. Perhaps you see a flower. Guide him into a position in which his face is close to the flower and gently touch his nose. After he smells the flower, you may want to tap next to an eye so that he will have the opportunity to look at it. As you continue the walk, you might notice that the leaves of a huge oak are dancing in the wind. You can bring your child under the tree, carefully tilt his head back, and signal him to open his eyes and witness the tree from this unusual angle. After a few moments continue on the journey. Perhaps you are near a stream. You can bring him to the bank, tap his ear to invite him to listen to the song of the brook, and then gently put his hand into the stream so he can feel the cool, wet touch of the water. As you move on, you may find yourself noticing the smallest details. You might see an ant climbing up the bark of a tree, and you can share this with your child. Or you may come upon a tiny wild strawberry and offer him an extraordinary burst of flavor. After about ten minutes of leading your child on the Wonder Walk, switch roles and let him lead you. (But make sure that neither of you puts something in the other's mouth unless you know that it's edible!)

The Wonder Walk can be life altering. It is as if one is meeting the natural world for the first time. Such an activity can utterly transform a child who is frightened of nature, who is scared of bugs, who is uncomfortable in her body, or who is addicted to television or video games. It can turn a child who litters as a matter of course into one who wants to live more carefully and more respectfully.

I have done this activity with inner city kids, corporate executives, scientists, activists, small children, teenagers, the elderly, and those for whom trust comes slowly. For some it is frightening to close their eyes and rely on a partner. To have such intimacy both with one's partner and with nature itself can sometimes be overwhelming, yet the vast majority of people experience a kind of grace when doing this simple activity, and their reverence is awakened.

I adore doing the Wonder Walk with Forest, and he loves to Wonder Walk me and his dad. One day when he was six, Forest and I were hiking in a Maine coast forest where the sea fog moistens the woods so that moss grows over the forest floor like a rich, green carpet and climbs up the tree trunks like emerald drapery. It was a sunny day, but we were deep in the shade of the woods under the canopy of trees. Forest led me to a spot where a ray of sunlight hit the forest floor. He carefully positioned me so that I was lying on the trail with my head resting on a soft bed of moss. He let me lie there for a few moments while the warm sun bathed my skin. When he tapped next to my eyes, it was his beautiful face that I saw first. That moment was so precious, and our connection to one another and to the earth so deep, that I thought I had never before been so happy.

Imagine if all children did such activities with their parents, with their friends, with their grandparents, with their siblings, with their classmates, and with their teachers. Imagine what a different world we might have if we all took a brief time to be together in nature in such a way. Try the Wonder Walk with your children and see what happens. Chances are, while you are busy falling in love with the Earth, you will connect more deeply with each other. Chances are that after the Wonder Walk you will both find it easier to make choices that protect the Earth because your heart will be filled with love and awe for the miraculous planet that is our home and provides our sustenance. Chances are that falling in love with nature will more deeply inspire your compassion.

OTHER IDEAS TO INSPIRE REVERENCE FOR NATURE

- Just to repeat: simply bring your children outside as often as possible. *Make outdoor activities routine rather than rare.*
- Plant a garden. Your toddler will enjoy being by your side, looking at bugs and worms, feeling and smelling the soil and flowers, and eating the fruits of your labor. If you don't have a backyard or access to a community garden, you can still plant herbs in window boxes.
- Consider a camping trip instead of heading to Disney World, Sea World, or Six Flags on vacation. Children love to sleep in tents, hear the sounds of the night, see the stars, be close to their parents and siblings, and have unstructured time in the day to just play and be.
- Check out books by Joseph Cornell and others who describe fun and inspiring outdoor activities you can do with children (see the Resources section for further reading).
- Find out what's available in your neighborhood. It's likely that there are nature centers nearby, and most have activities designed for young children.
- You can bring reverence for nature inside, too, by doing projects with natural materials. Pine needles, sea glass and shells, leaves and pieces of bark, dried beans, fragrant herbs and silky milkweed can all become the raw ingredients for your children's imagination and creativity. (Be careful not to remove living things such as moss, bark that is still on live trees, etc.) You can make dyes from goldenrod and teas from herbs. In engaging in these activities, you feed not only your children's creative spirits, but also your own.

Your children, delighting in their creations, will also learn to give birthday and holiday gifts from their hearts and hands, rather than from the mall. There are wonderful books that teach how to do natural crafts with children, which you can find at your local library (see also the Resources section).

There are many who will read these suggestions and feel weighed down by the effort, in both time and expertise, that such activities entail. For many working parents, there is barely enough time to pop a frozen entree into the microwave for dinner, let alone to grow and prepare whole foods or go on a camping trip. We may feel inadequate to provide either trips to the wilderness or art projects from nature. In fact, we ourselves may be a bit biophobic, scared to step too far into the woods. Still, every choice we make in the direction of promoting reverence for nature makes a difference. We can take small steps toward a more wonder-filled life.

PROTECTING AND NOURISHING OUR CHILDREN'S SOULS

Protecting and nourishing our children's bodies is an obvious task for parents, but protecting and nourishing their souls is just as essential. Shielding them from values you don't admire and offering them the values you do can be a struggle in a profit-driven culture where the message of materialism is so ubiquitous.

When our family moved to Maine, we didn't immediately notice that the state does not permit billboards. It wasn't until we left Maine on trips to other states that we realized how bombarded we had previously been with billboard advertising. Billboards had been inescapable, and we had been subjected to countless images of people smoking and drinking or advertisements with women (and sometimes men) in provocative poses. Our son had grown up through his toddler years seeing these images regularly, and we'd barely even noticed. Most of us have become unaware of the many media messages that surround us.

TELEVISION AND VIDEOS

As our children grow up and become school age, we can invite them to become critical consumers, but the young child's heart and mind are porous, vulnerable, and innocent and need to be shielded from inappropriate or harmful messages. Yet it is difficult to know how to fight the inexorable tentacles of corporate messages reaching into our children's minds and hearts since these messages are virtually everywhere. While it's impossible to protect our children from all media messages, however, we can significantly limit the media that they receive during their early years — and the best place to start is by limiting or turning off the television. While children's programming on public television is usually benign and sometimes positive, commercial television can be damaging to our children's young minds and hearts. So many children's television shows are filled with images of violence, cruelty, and cynicism that flash by at an astounding rate. There is no time for a child to understand, ponder, or respond to what they are witnessing. Children watching television are at the mercy of those images. What happens on the screen is happening, in some sense, to them, right in their own homes. We may not be able to see their hearts racing, nor realize from their passive faces that they are being deeply influenced by the images and words that they are experiencing, but whether we can see it or not, our children *are* being affected by whatever media images they are exposed to.

The advertising during commercial children's television (and more and more during the underwriter's "ads" on public television as well) is even faster than the programming itself. It is a visual and auditory kaleidoscope, and millions of children sit immobile as these images and words convince them to "need" countless products, often with ferocious desire. It's important to ask yourself if you want your child to be the receptive audience for carefully crafted commercial messages. Most of the products advertised on TV are not healthy for our children, either physically or spiritually, and the underlying messages may not be the ones that you most want to inspire and instill in your child.

There are many books about the negative impact of television on our ability to think our own thoughts and feel our own emotions, and they are worth reading before you decide to let your young child watch television routinely (see the Resources section for book suggestions). Television may not be uniformly bad, but can you trust corporations that are motivated to sell advertising space (to other corporations that want to sell products) to have the best interests of your children in mind when they produce a children's show? As a parent you can ask yourself this: Am I creating an environment for my young child that is most conducive to helping her become the best that she can be? Am I helping her mind, heart, and soul to thrive? Am I nourishing her innocent spirit with the qualities I want her to embody? And does commercial television help or hinder me in my effort to create a positive and humane environment for her?

What about videos? Let's consider just one Disney film, *Beauty and the Beast*, and analyze it a bit to discover what messages are being offered to our children. This classic story was turned into a film that includes messages about what it means to be good and faithful, loving and compassionate. Belle, the film's protagonist, is a bright, independent, and compassionate young woman. She is not easily impressed by good looks or big muscles. So far so good. But Belle is imprisoned by an abusive "Beast" with whom she eventually falls in love. Her love and goodness tame and transform the "Beast," and when they kiss, she frees the prince inside.

It's worth asking whether young boys are subtly taught by this film to expect girls to endure their rage and anger, and whether young girls are taught to be patient and loving to the suffering boy who, through her devotion, will eventually be changed into a prince. Are these the messages we want to teach girls and boys when we have so many women who stay in abusive relationships believing that their partners will one day change, and so many men who abuse their wives and girlfriends? Patience, kindness, and compassion *are* virtues, but tolerating abuse is not virtuous, and it's worth asking whether it serves young children to be exposed to such a message.

I am not suggesting that children's entertainment ought to be sanitized and sappy. Plenty of children's stories are filled with grim and complex characters and plots, and they help children to grapple with fear and find courage, to understand the difficulties in struggling against the worst of human qualities in favor of the best. But most of these stories are not really meant for very young children. Many films which can be discussed with older children cannot be analyzed with a three-year-old. Instead, the three-year-old simply absorbs the messages and values. To many parents a G-rating means that the toddler can watch, too. We cannot assume, however, that the classic cartoons or the newest G-rated film is good for our young children. It is worth seeing the film first, and thinking carefully about the messages and images contained in it, before sitting our children down in front of the video and allowing someone else to be their role model.

Even when films have positive messages and are relatively benign, they may still constrain our children's play. When Forest was young, he loved to watch *The Land Before Time* videos. Within a short time, however, he was mimicking the characters in the films and wanted to reenact the story lines with his friends. There is not necessarily anything wrong with this. The stories included humane lessons, yet there was something disconcerting about watching our son act out another person's story over and over or chatter with a cartoon character's voice day after day. Where was his imagination in this reenactment?

If you have been allowing your child to watch television and videos, and this section has made you rethink that decision, you may be wondering how you can change your family's habits now. I wondered this, too. Although I prided myself on being a very conscious parent around certain issues, I'd used videos as a blessed "babysitter" from the time Forest was two. By the time he was in kindergarten, he'd watched numerous films. One evening, his teacher, a woman I admire tremendously, hosted a parent-teacher meeting at school. When I walked into Forest's classroom, she was sitting in front of a television. She showed us selections from four videos — *The Lion King*, *The Wizard of Oz*, *Star Wars*, and a *Goosebumps* video — and asked us to consider whether such videos were appropriate for our kindergarten-aged children. The selections she played, shown in this different light, were shocking. I realized that *The Lion King* was terribly violent (depicting fratricide and blaming a child for the death of his father), *The Wizard of Oz* had terrifying moments, *Star Wars* included, not surprisingly, many scenes of *war*, and the *Goosebumps* video was horribly scary at any age. Forest had already seen the first three of these films! "Now what?" I thought. I knew it wouldn't be easy to put an end to what had become routine video-watching. I went home, talked to my husband, and we sorted through the videos in the house. We put away most of them and spoke to Forest in the morning. We told him that his teacher, whom he loved and respected, had told us that a lot of the videos he had been watching were really not good for young children's minds and hearts and that we weren't going to watch these videos any more until he was older. I was sure that Forest would be argumentative and angry. He surprised me when he seemed to accept our new rules without much complaint. As I thought about this acceptance over the years, I came to the conclusion that Forest didn't fight us because he could sense that we were making a decision based on our deep love and commitment to doing the very best for him.

TOYS

I don't want to sound like a spoil sport, but toys often come at a hefty price (far in excess of the actual price tag). For example, let's examine the phenomenon of stuffed animals. Stuffed animals have been around for generations, but in recent years, they have been marketed as collectibles, meaning that it's not good enough to have a couple of beloved stuffed animals — you must have dozens. How many stuffed animals do our children need before they cannot cherish any because they are no longer precious and special? Showering our children with such toys does not really serve them, and these toys come at a cost to others around the globe. They are usually produced in other countries, often through sweatshop labor. Their raw materials, production, transportation, and distribution use up fossil fuels and eventually they wind up in landfills and incinerators.

Both we and our children have become the target audience for a massive market in cheaply made, disposable toys. Our children have more and more toys with less and less reverence and appreciation for them. When a new children's film comes out, the market is saturated with cheap spin-off dolls, most of which quickly end up in the trash. When you buy your children toys, try to remind yourself to buy what really serves them and does not cause harm to others.

Before you make a toy purchase, you can ask yourself the following questions:

- Will the toy help nourish my child's true self and spirit?
- Will the toy or game contribute to a positive, friendly experience of play for my child and his playmates?
- Is it poorly made and likely to wind up in a landfill or incinerator before long, contributing to the pollution of my child's world?
- Does it really reflect our family's values?
- Is the toy I'm about to buy my own child produced by another child working in a sweatshop?
- Did its production cause harm to animals?
- Does the toy promote violent play?
- Could I organize a hand-me-down toy party with friends whose children are of different ages?

- Does the toy foster creative play?
- Could we make more toys ourselves?

As you answer these questions for yourself, you'll create your own criteria and guidelines for toy purchases and have more clarity around what choices you want to make when it comes to toys for your child.

INSTILLING REVERENCE FOR THE GOOD

Limiting television and carefully choosing videos and toys is all well and good, but what will you do to replace these easy forms of entertainment? Moreover, what can you do to actually inspire reverence for people and actions that are good? Here are a few suggestions:

- Read stories to your young children about noble, kind, and compassionate protagonists, inspiring their reverence and appreciation for characters with character.
- Share your own family stories about good and courageous people who are friends, neighbors, or relatives.
- Let your child know what you appreciate about him. When he does or says something that inspires your reverence, tell him.
- Start an appreciation ritual. Before dinner have each person who is old enough say one thing for which they are grateful.
- Expand your appreciation ritual to include a once-a-week expression of thanks for something that each person in the family did that week.
- Treat simple tasks with reverence. When the herbs that come from the window box are placed reverently in the soup pot, an ordinary chore becomes an act filled with meaning, joy, and abiding gratitude.
- Surround your child with people you revere. Expand the role models in your child's life to include those whom you

most respect and admire. Consider asking a couple of these people to be mentors to your child. You can invite those adults whom you consider to be wise, loving, and compassionate to formally take on a role in your child's life, a role similar to that of godparents in the Christian tradition.

- Choose to do community service that your child can participate in. When your child sees the benefits of your generosity and volunteerism, he learns to appreciate the joy that such service brings to the giver as well as the many gifts it brings to the recipients.

WHAT TO DO WHEN ...

In each of these developmental chapters, I've included a "What to do when" box that explores how you might handle a common problem during a particular stage in your child's life. While each of these boxes focuses on a specific problem, they are meant to demonstrate how you might respond to any dilemma using the Four Elements. However, these boxes won't actually tell what to say or what decision to make. Instead, they will show you the kinds of questions you may want to ask, and help you understand how to use the Four Elements to decide for yourself what is right for you and your child when faced with a difficult issue or dilemma.

WHAT TO DO WHEN
YOUR FIVE-YEAR-OLD SON WANTS A TOY GUN

a) Give yourself time to respond

Let your son know you will think about it and get back to him. Explain that you don't want to make a quick decision without giving it some careful thought.

b) Element 1: Gather information

Perhaps you already know what you think about toy guns, or maybe you thought you knew but now that your child is begging for a toy gun, you're not so sure. In order to make a decision that best reflects your values, you can gather information about the impact of toy guns on children's play, read books or articles, ask other parents whom you respect, and review commentaries on the Internet. It's also important to gather information from your son. You can ask him, "Why do you want a toy gun? What will you use it for?" By asking questions, you will be in a better position to evaluate his desires and needs and to figure out what is best for him and your family. Perhaps there are other ways to satisfy the needs he is expressing.

c) Element 2: Think critically

Sit down with the information, sort through it, and weigh the opinions you've gathered along with your own beliefs. Whatever decision you ultimately make, let it come from an informed, thoughtful place. Not only will you feel better about a decision that has come from careful deliberation, your son will also know that you are trying to make the best choice for him.

d) Element 3: Use the three Rs

As you consider how to nurture your child's reverence, instill respect, and teach responsibility, think about whether or not a toy gun will help or hinder you in your efforts. Consider ways in which either decision can be used to help instill the three Rs. For example, if you say yes to the toy gun, you can still create rules and expectations that help your child play with it in a respectful and responsible way. If you say no to it, you might share your views on guns so that your son's awareness is further awakened. You can also develop guidelines for pretend guns made from sticks or fingers so that such play won't diminish the three Rs either.

e) Element 4: Make the most positive choice

Make a decision that reflects your values and represents the most positive choice for your child and your family. Explain to your son why you made the decision you did so that he will understand how you used your best judgment to make a decision in his best interest.

f) Stay flexible and be willing to revisit the issue

Be open to reconsidering the issue and perhaps changing your mind. That's what happened in our family. My husband and I decided not to get Forest a toy gun during the early years although he asked for one many times. We still faced the issue of gun play because he turned sticks into weapons, so we made guidelines around this play and insisted that he not point pretend weapons at people or animals. We were forced to revisit our decision about toy guns when Forest was seven and he won a plastic water pistol at a fair before we could intervene and ask for a different prize. We decided that taking his prize away would be worse for Forest than modifying our earlier decision, and we decided to let him keep the water gun.

You, too, may find that your opinion changes over time. You might decide to get your child a toy gun, and then realize later that your son is behaving in a more violent and aggressive way with it than you want. You may then want to modify your decision.

STORY TELLING AND STORY CREATION

My friend Nancy Mellon is a master storyteller, but more importantly she teaches people how to tell their own stories. The first time I met her, I had a few minutes to ask her a question about Forest who was five at the time. I shared with her some struggles Forest was having and asked her advice. She offered me the beginning of a story that I might tell my son. I couldn't wait to try. I was apprehensive, though. What if the story didn't come to me? What if I couldn't flesh it out? What if it was uninteresting? What if I couldn't figure out an ending? You see, Nancy doesn't teach how to write stories and then read them, she teaches how to open up to receiving a story in the very moment that one is sharing it. It takes trust and faith to tell such a story.

That night I lit a candle in Forest's room, sat in the rocking chair by his bed, took a deep breath, and began. The story spilled out of me, and it captivated Forest. When it was over, he looked at me with shining eyes and, with so much sincerity and appreciation, whispered, "*Thanks*, Mama." Since then I have been periodically creating stories for Forest around the same characters.

These stories aren't just entertaining; they are soul enriching. The characters and their adventures come out of my spirit for the sole benefit of Forest's spirit. They are offered to him as a gift for his own journey and struggles. They speak directly to him because they are meant for him. This kind of storytelling has not only been a blessing for Forest, it has been important for me. I a way to connect with and help my son not through giving or passive listening (which are important, too), but through creatively touching his very soul. Even on those nights when I feared I had no story in me, or when I thought I was too tired to come up with anything, if I closed my eyes and opened myself up to the unknown, the story would come. In fact, it was usually on those nights when I felt most tired and uncreative that the best stories arrived.

You, too, can create stories for your child. They can be woven from your imagination as well as your deepest values. These stories will serve your children's spirits in ways that television, movies, and even books cannot. There will be no pictures but those that arise from the children's own minds and hearts, no story line that some stranger invented, no products that some company wants to sell, no consumption that someone tries to promote.

Nancy Mellon has two books which will help you learn how to begin this beautiful journey into storytelling: *The Art of Storytelling* and *Storytelling for Children*. These will get you started on a path that will lead you and your children into unknown and extraordinary territory in which you get to lay the very best foundation for raising your child to be humane through engaging her with your own creativity and sharing with her your deepest values.

FIVE

THE MIDDLE YEARS
(AGES 7-12)

... we cannot inculcate values, such as generosity, compassion, non-harming, equality, and appreciation for diversity through moralizing or coercion. We can advocate for them, however, but ultimately, it is through embodying these values ourselves that our children come to have a direct experience of them and absorb them into their view of themselves and the world.

— MYLA AND JON KABAT-ZINN

D URING THE MIDDLE YEARS, children are developmentally prepared to grapple with ethics. They are generally drawn toward stories with heroic characters and love books in which good triumphs over evil. Their consciences are awake, and they are often very receptive to those people (including parents and teachers as well as fictional characters) who would encourage nobility. Often very eager to be their best, they look to respected adults for truth and clarity.

If the early years are the time to build a strong foundation, it is during the middle years that you will actually build the house, laying the bricks of humane values so that your child will know how to live with kindness and respect. While you are doing this, however, be aware that your children will also be influenced by "houses" other than your own, both literally and figuratively. As they grow up during the middle years, their beliefs and ideas will begin to come less from you and more from their peer group. As school culture takes hold, children will usually find in their peers an ethos that speaks to them and answers their questions about who and how to be. This peer culture may carry significant weight, molding your children's ideas and perspectives and shaping their values.

As children are exposed to more and more media during the middle years of childhood, the greater culture also begins to exert a growing influence. Even if you continue to shield your children from too much television or inappropriate films, their friends who are exposed to these media may tell them more than you might want them to know. Your own values may be threatened by the messages that surround your still young child.

Your children will also face more social challenges. They will almost certainly be exposed to bullying, cheating, or stealing, and they may themselves become either a victim or a perpetrator of these behaviors (and sometimes both). They may face the fear of ostracism, and at times, the desperate desire to fit in. They will need to learn to understand and cope with subtle manipulation and deceit among their classmates.

Much has been written about the trials of adolescence, but the challenges of the middle years, especially as children approach junior high, can be considerable. It is not easy at the best of times to be humane, to make kind, compassionate, and wise choices in life. During the middle years, children may face significant obstacles on the path toward humane decision-making. There will likely be moments when they despise their own behavior but feel impotent to stop themselves from acting ignobly at best and cruelly at worst. Consider the following story about Alisa, a woman I've known for years, who discovered when she was twelve that she could be quite cruel.

ALISA AND ARIANNA

When she was a girl, Alisa went to camp for several weeks each summer. In general she liked summer camp and had made some good friends, but there was one girl in her bunk named Sabina who was routinely mean to her. Sabina was very popular, so Alisa tried as hard as she could to get along with her. She was afraid that she would be excluded if she didn't find a way to stay in Sabina's good graces. But Sabina didn't like Alisa and frequently talked about Alisa behind her back. Alisa would hear about this from her friends in the bunk, but she tried not to say anything mean about Sabina because she was afraid that her friends might feel forced to choose sides and might choose Sabina instead of her. Each summer Alisa came to camp resolved to get along with Sabina, and one summer on the first day of camp she even said to Sabina, "I know we haven't gotten along that well, but I'd really like to be friends." Sabina sneered at her and evasively responded, "I don't know what you're talking about." Inside, Alisa was enraged. She hated Sabina, and she despised the way she groveled in order to stay in Sabina's circle. She also hated it that her other friends liked Sabina, and she was frustrated by her own powerlessness.

The summer that Alisa turned twelve, there was a new girl in the bunk, Arianna, who was very shy, quiet, and extremely modest.

While all the other girls changed their clothes by their beds, Arianna would slip into the bathroom to undress. One day after rest hour, Arianna picked up her bathing suit and began walking to the bathroom. Sabina and a few other girls started shouting at her to just change her clothes like everyone else. "What are you trying to hide, Arianna?" they jeered. Arianna turned crimson and looked like a trapped animal. She said that she preferred to change in privacy. Alisa joined in, asking "Why? Is there something wrong with you?" With that Alisa and two other girls lifted up Arianna's shirt, laughing at her.

When the girls finally stopped tormenting Arianna, she ran sobbing to the bathroom. Alisa was deeply ashamed of herself. She had discovered how cruel she could be.

Unfortunately, the middle years of childhood are a time when peer pressures, teasing, and bullying make stories like Alisa's all too common. Children enter school and discover that social relationships are fraught with complications. Today's best friend may turn on them tomorrow. There are kids to be avoided on the playground or placated for safety's sake. Otherwise well-adjusted children like Alisa can become heartless. Cliques and gangs form and expect allegiance. The consequence of rejecting the power dynamics may be exclusion at best and persecution at worst. Children often lose their grip on their deepest values, and virtues such as compassion, kindness, and courage may be eclipsed by anxiety that turns into cowardice and cruelty. Following the crowd may become so compelling that the desire to live and act humanely loses its hold.

How can incidences like the one described above be prevented? What could Alisa's parents have done differently so Alisa might not have taken out her fear and rage on Arianna? What had happened to Alisa to make her act so mean?

MODELING THE MESSAGE DURING
THE MIDDLE YEARS

Alisa's father was, himself, a bully. While his behavior does not necessarily explain Alisa's actions (and certainly doesn't excuse her treatment of Arianna), it seems more than a coincidence that Alisa grew up as the victim of her father's rage and later acted in a similar way. Alisa's mother was loving and gentle but completely preoccupied with her own life. She was also afraid of her husband and didn't come to Alisa's rescue when he went on a tirade against their daughter. Alisa's father regularly gossiped about people, referring to the woman across the street as "the fat sow."

I spoke to Alisa many years after the incident at camp. She told me about that summer, and I asked her why she thought she had been so cruel to Arianna. "I really don't know. Something just overcame me, and I didn't think about what I was doing. In that moment I was part of the powerful group, and I was almost high on that power. I wasn't a victim any more. I was in control."

I asked Alisa what might have prevented her from doing what she did to Arianna, and she responded, "If I'd had a shred of self-esteem, I don't think I would have participated in the incident. In fact, I think I would have tried to stop it because most of the time I was very high-minded about what was good or bad. But I was too afraid, and in that moment right and wrong disappeared and were replaced with either being the one with power or being a victim. I had been the victim of Sabina's mocking cruelty for years, and I'd swallowed it and sucked up to her, desperate for the crumbs of her occasional good will. For a few minutes I actually enjoyed being mean like her."

I asked Alisa how she thought her parents could have raised her differently so that she might not have been so cruel to Arianna.

"I think the biggest thing missing from my childhood was the sense that kindness matters. My dad was always talking behind people's backs, always insulting people, always blaming others, and I started to do that, too. I didn't do it out loud that much, but I certainly did it inside. I didn't really think that it was important to show respect to everyone, only to people with power. My parents didn't encourage me to think about others' feelings growing up. They were very competitive. I knew I had to succeed no matter what, and that success, whether at school or sports, could come at almost any price."

Had Alisa's parents stressed kindness over competition, had her father modeled respect instead of disdain for others, had Alisa's mother protected her daughter and demonstrated courage in the face of fear, perhaps Alisa would have found ways of working through her own fears and insecurities instead of bullying Arianna.

So much of what our children learn about human interactions comes from how well we model healthy, respectful, and loving relationships for them. If children hear us badmouthing others, they learn that this is acceptable. If they observe us abandoning a friend in need, out of fear or discomfort, they will not be able to witness the courage of intimacy. If they see us snubbing certain people, they may learn to be snobs. Our children will discover from us how to be a good friend, how to be loyal and kind, how to be committed and brave — if we model such virtues for them in our own relationships. They will then also learn to be kind in all relationships, regardless of whether or not they call someone a friend.

Our children will also learn how to extend kindness beyond their small community of friends and family by watching us. As we extend our compassion and care for others outside of our neighborhood, we will help them to break out of the confining world of peer and cultural influences and allow them to meet truly important needs that will give them a wider perspective on life. In itself that perspective often helps them negotiate the difficulties that arise in their peer group because they have meaningful goals to offset the often shallow values that may surround them.

THE FOUR ELEMENTS DURING
THE MIDDLE YEARS

Just when our children are becoming ever more susceptible to powerful peer and cultural influences and are emerging into a challenging time in their social development, they are also ready for more of the Four Elements described in Chapter 2. Because they are developmentally prepared to explore morality and are usually very interested in determining right and wrong and being noble themselves, the Four Elements work very well during these years. In age-appropriate ways you can begin to rely upon the Four Elements to help your child both maintain and further develop humane values.

ELEMENT 1: PROVIDING INFORMATION

As your children grow up during the middle years, you can provide more and more information to enable them to make humane choices. When and how should you furnish this information? Often, external events will provide the impetus for sharing information. Let's consider bullying again. If your child is a witness to bullying, you can talk to him about why someone might bully someone else. You can let your child know that often bullies have themselves been victims of bullying. People who bully others are usually insecure, angry, and scared, even though they may sometimes appear to be in charge and powerful. Providing this information is not meant to excuse bullying, but to put it into a perspective that can help your child understand how and why violence is perpetuated, and to offer insight into how it might be stopped. It's important that your child understand that not only the victims of bullying need help but the bully needs help, too. If your child has witnessed bullying that no adult has seen, providing this information may help your child understand the necessity to tell the teacher. If you call the teacher yourself, you empower your child to report bullying in the future, perhaps while it is happening. The next step might be a class meeting resulting in a new focus in the classroom on kindness and respect.

Other than modeling, one of the best ways to prevent your own child from becoming a bully or being unkind and ungenerous in general is to provide information about those who are suffering in order to extend your child's compassion and empathy. It's amazing how far a bit of awareness can go toward building character. When a child learns that there are boys his age who are forced to work sixteen hours a day at brick factories in Asia, he gains a perspective that can foster altruism and care. If your family then sponsors a child in Asia or donates money to an organization such as Free the Children (which works to stop such exploitation of children), your child realizes that there is something that he can do to help, which nurtures his compassion and generosity. I cannot stress enough, however, how important it is to share information about suffering only in age-appropriate ways. Although I've defined the middle years as ages 7-12, seven is not some magic year when it's time to expose your child to the ills of the world. If you are unsure about whether some news story, some tragedy, or some knowledge about someone else's suffering might be more than your child can or should bear, please err on the side of protecting your child. But while it's important to protect your child from too much information too soon, we live in a culture that often makes many children quite self-absorbed and self-centered; these traits in turn tend to inhibit them from being humane because they may rarely think of others. Bringing to their awareness the plight of children around the world may be exactly what they need to become more compassionate.

If you are making choices to live more humanely, if you are consciously choosing humanely produced clothes and organic foods, it is during the middle years of childhood that you can begin to share with your children your reasons for making these choices. Providing the background information on companies you've chosen to boycott and products you're refusing to buy, and sharing information about the products you are picking instead, will help your child understand the power of daily choices to improve the world and help others. If children understand that using paper cups means the destruction of trees, the loss of habitat for wildlife, the pollution of water through chlorine bleaching, and the despoiling of the planet through trash production, they may choose glass instead. If they understand that drinking soda is not only unhealthy for them, but also contributes to destructive bauxite mining for aluminum, significant fuel consumption in aluminum production, possible poisoning of waterways from the toxic inks used to label cans, and inevitable oil spills and wildlife deaths through obtaining ever more fossil fuels to ship carbonated sugar water throughout the world, they may more often choose tap water instead of Coke or Pepsi, or at least not argue with you if you decide not to buy soda. They will not always make the most humane choices (nor will you), but with information they will at least have the knowledge to begin assessing their decisions and to further manifest kindness and compassion.

ELEMENT 2: TEACHING CRITICAL THINKING

"But everyone else gets to!" How many times have you heard this refrain, or some variation on the theme? Even if you are living a life that in most respects is similar to that of your neighbors and reflects the dominant values of our culture, your child will probably utter this phrase more than once. Most of the time it is easy enough to simply explain to your child that sometimes you make different choices for her than other parents make for their children, but if you are going to raise your child to eat humane foods, wear humane clothes, and use humane products, if you are going to make an expansive understanding of compassion and kindness the overarching principles for your family, then it's likely that your child will have a lifestyle that differs from many of her peers. Using critical thinking techniques will help your child understand why you've made certain decisions as well as empower her to make her own humane choices.

Critical thinking tips for the middle years

- Teach your child to be a product sleuth. During the middle years, most children like to be investigators. They take pride in their ability to understand new information and make clever connections and decisions. When you go shopping, teach your child how to read labels. You might show them how to sleuth out sugar, artificial ingredients, organic versus nonorganic foods, whole foods versus refined ones, and a number of other criteria that are important to you. You can also show them how to find the cruelty-free logo and the words "Not animal tested" on personal care products, or phrases like "Fair trade" on chocolate and coffee. The critical thinking element comes into play when you teach your child to read product packaging with a critical eye. "All Natural," "Low-Fat," and "Healthy" may appear on the packaging, but are these claims backed up by the actual ingredients? By teaching your child how to answer this question, you will be raising a critical thinker.

- When you're driving and you see a billboard, engage your child's mind in analyzing the message. You might ask, "Why do you think that cigarette ad shows beautiful young people having fun at the beach?" Having provided information to them about the health hazards of smoking, you can encourage them to look carefully at the billboard for any evidence of smoking's ill effects. When they don't find any, ask them what they're "taught" by the advertisement instead. As you teach your child to be aware and alert, you invite them to explore their own values and feel empowered to be wise thinkers.

- If you allow your child to watch television, watch with her and ask her questions to help her think critically about both the shows themselves and the commercials. Rather than allow her to be a passive viewer, teach her how to analyze what she sees in order to understand the ways in which she is being manipulated to want certain products or lifestyles.

- If you do not allow your child to watch television, especially during the first few of the middle years, explain very clearly why you are making a decision that is different from what other families do. Help him to think critically about the impact of television on young minds and about how time spent watching television is time that is unavailable to do other, more enriching and meaningful things. Through fostering critical thinking you can help him join you enthusiastically in your choices rather than feel like a victim of your values.

- Teach your child to be a CRITIC. Professor Wayne Bartz has come up with a method to teach students to be critical thinkers. CRITIC stands for **C**laim? **R**ole of the claimant? **I**nformation backing the claim? **T**est? **I**ndependent testing? **C**ause proposed? Here's how the CRITIC technique might work in practice: Imagine that your daughter has seen an advertisement for a diet shake that promises to make her lose weight. You can explain how to use the CRITIC method to analyze the ad. First, one could teach her to name and describe the claim itself (*You can lose weight by consuming our diet shake*). Next, ask her, "Who is making the claim, and is there something in it for them if you believe the claim?" (*The company will make money by selling diet shakes if people believe the claim.*) Then ask her if there is any evidence offered in support of the claim (*The ad has a testimonial and before-and-after photos of a woman who says she drank the diet shake*). If there is any reason one might doubt the claim, ask her whether a test could be designed to prove or disprove the claim (*People who drink the diet shake could be compared to people on different diets*). The next question to ask is whether there has been any independent testing to prove or disprove the claim (*Has any researcher not connected to the company and with no vested interest in the* *outcome tested the diet plan?*). Lastly, help your daughter analyze whether the claimant has proposed a cause to explain why the claim is true (*How and why would people lose weight drinking the diet shake?*). Learning a simple method like CRITIC will empower your child to become skeptical of claims and seek out truth as a matter of course.

Having these skills doesn't mean your child won't want the latest product, but it does mean that he'll be able to pause and assess it, and make a more informed decision before spending his allowance on something he won't want in two months. Good critical thinking skills will also help your child if your family simply cannot afford the newest trend. Rather than feel deprived, your child may feel good about himself if he is able to clearly assess the product's true value and finds it lacking.

ELEMENT 3: INSTILLING THE THREE Rs

When you think about what you might like your child to experience during the middle years, some of the following experiences may capture your imagination and make you want to find a way to bring them, or something like them, to your children:

- Witnessing dragonflies emerge from their nymph stage and dry off in the sun before taking flight
- Watching hummingbirds visit the flowers in your window box
- Seeing a beaver swim silently by in the moonlight
- Climbing a mountain
- Swimming in a canyon pool carved out by a river
- Listening to a teenager tell his story about overcoming tremendous adversity and working to bring justice to his community
- Attending a talk by an elder Native American who describes the traditional Indian life that used to exist in

your region

- Participating in a community event to raise money for a local homeless shelter
- Attending weekly religious services that promote humane values and actions

It is wondrous experiences in nature and meaningful inspiration from other people that your children can call upon when they are confused about who they are and what is important in life. These are grounding, deeply satisfying experiences that teach our children that they are part of a miracle and can be part of creating peace and justice in the world. Such experiences strengthen their will to protect and respect this planet and all who reside here. It is so important that during the middle years we offer our children wonder-filled and enriching experiences over and over again. There may come a time, perhaps sooner than you think, when they may not want to join you on a camping trip or at a community event. We parents have a relatively small window of opportunity to actively share the beauty of the world and the wisdom of humane people with our growing children before they will decide for themselves what they will do with their time. When we spark their reverence, we kindle their respect and light the fire for future responsible citizenship.

Reverence for nature

There are opportunities to experience the wonder of nature all around us if we pay attention. For example, in November 2001, many people in the United States were privileged to see a spectacular display of the Leonid meteor showers. Watching the Leonids required getting up in the middle of the night and finding a location that was not polluted by bright city lights or blocked by trees or big buildings. We have friends who arose with their seven- and nine-year-old boys at 3 a.m. and hiked up a nearby mountain with flashlights in order to watch the meteors.

When they got to the top of the small mountain, there were many other people who had done the same thing. Together they watched hundreds of shooting stars lighting up the sky like fireworks. No movie, no television show, no book, no computer game, and no class could have taken the place of those meteor shows. The children who were brought to see this wondrous event in the night sky will likely never forget it. As they grow up, if light pollution creeps into their towns, suburbs, and small cities, they may speak out to protect the starry sky from too many bright lights. Their early reverence can pave the way for future responsible stewardship.

Nature games

There are activities we can do in nature that require little more than a few trees, a backyard, and some cloth for blindfolds; these activities can instill reverence under the guise of play. Here are two games to get you started. (If your children enjoy them, you can find many more activities in books listed in the Resources section.)

Smell Teas
Bring together a group of no more than five children and give each a cup. Explain that each of them will be making a "smell" tea from natural objects. Invite them to fill their cup with soil, leaves, flowers, herbs, pine needles, or berries (but *not* water) and have them stir their smell tea with a stick. Then tell them to give their tea a name. When all the teas are prepared and named, have each child pass around his tea and tell its name so that everyone has a chance to share their concoction before playing the Smell Tea game.

To play the game, have one person be "it" and put on a blindfold. One at a time each member of the group should place a tea in the person's hands. The person who's "it" smells the tea and guesses it by name. Once he has had the chance to smell each tea and guess its name, the next person gets to be "it" and the game continues until everyone has had a chance to test their nose.

The Smell Tea game not only awakens our sense of smell, it usually elicits marvel at the variety of aromas that can be created using many of the same raw ingredients. More often than not, each tea is very distinct and easy to identify even though the participants have gathered natural objects from the same area. The game also builds memory skills and creativity and is a lot of fun.

Find Your Tree
To do this activity, you'll need to find some woods or a park with many trees. Participants pair up, and one of the pair puts on a blindfold. The other carefully leads her partner on a roundabout journey to a tree the partner picks out for her to "meet." The blindfolded child (or adult) feels the tree thoroughly, as high as she can reach, down at the base of the trunk, and around the perimeter. When she thinks she knows her tree, her partner leads her back (also in a roundabout way) to where she started. The blindfold comes off, and her job is to find her tree.

What a sense of accomplishment when she finds her tree (and most do on the first guess) and realizes how much she knows from her senses! That tree will never be quite the same to her. Perhaps it will become a place to explore, a place to rest, a place for contemplation, or a place for discovery.

Reverence for the good

It is not at all difficult to inspire a love of goodness during the middle years. The suggestions for inspiring reverence for the good from the last chapter apply during these years as well, but as your children get older, you can also include the following:

- Create a tradition, perhaps during dinner, where family members are invited to share any stories they have heard on the news or experienced in their day in which someone acted with particular virtue.

- Ask "What would you do?" in a variety of hypothetical or real situations. Invite your children to come up with the best solutions to complicated or difficult situations.
- Attend community events that bring out the best in people. These might include religious services, special Olympics-type sporting events, neighborhood caroling, community walks to raise money for worthy causes, etc.
- Attend talks with your children given by people whom you consider to be particularly wise, courageous, or compassionate.

Respect

Forest and I have a ritual. We have a spring-fed pond behind our house, and in the summer we lie on rafts and look at the frogs peppering the bank of the pond. Like most children, Forest wanted to pick up the frogs, and so I taught him how to hold his hand out in front of a frog, and to allow the frog to climb onto his palm. Some frogs have no interest, and these we leave alone, but other frogs climb onto our outstretched hands. Some hop right onto the raft. Sometimes Forest will float around the pond with three or four frogs on his raft. There's no doubt Forest experiences reverence for the frogs, but he has also learned to treat them with respect. Respect followed on the heels of his reverence.

Instilling respect for the natural world and for other species will actually help to inspire respect in other, unrelated and often difficult situations. Most children have an affinity for animals and nature. Other species are vulnerable and require our kindness if they are to survive. Helping children to respect those who are weaker and defenseless may help them respect other children who are unpopular or seemingly different, and will go far toward preventing incidences like the one that occurred between Alisa and Arianna. The converse is also true. Children who harm animals maliciously often grow up to be children who harm other people. It's critical to intervene and help these children. Often they are doing to other species what has been done to them, and recognizing this and interceding is crucial to breaking the cycle of violence.

Our children are growing up in a culture that often glorifies disrespect. They watch cartoons with rude heroes and hear insulting talk show hosts on the radio. They are growing up in a society in which corporate theft is becoming the norm. They are living in a nation in which politicians are assumed to lie. Children need to learn why such behaviors are not humane. They must understand the harm that is caused by deceit. Even when your own children are honest and respectful, they will still need your help to maintain their convictions and their virtues in today's world. Consider my young friend Cameron's story:

CAMERON, DENISE AND MARIAH

Cameron was at the local strip mall when she ran into her classmates Denise and Mariah. They were all in fifth grade, and were enjoying their new found freedom to be at the mall without their parents. Denise and Mariah were carrying shopping bags filled with stuff. They excitedly told Cameron they were ripping things off from shops and invited Cameron to join them at one of the big stores. Cameron didn't know what "ripping things off" meant, but she was too embarrassed to ask, and so she accompanied them to the store. When they went inside, Mariah whispered to her, "Just tell me if you see something you want." Suddenly, Cameron understood what her friends were doing. She made up an excuse and quickly left the store.

Cameron had never considered stealing from stores, and she was shocked not only that her friends were shoplifting, but also that they were bragging about it. She tried to figure out why they were stealing and why they didn't seem to think that what they were doing was wrong. Perhaps Denise, whose family didn't have much money, might feel she had to steal to get things she wanted, but she knew that Mariah's family was wealthy. They lived in a huge house in the fanciest development in town.

Cameron didn't know what to do. She was glad that she had a half-mile walk before she would get home because she needed time to think. She wasn't sure if she should tell her mother. What Denise and Mariah were doing was wrong, but telling on someone was also wrong. What would happen if they found out she'd told on them? By the time Cameron got home, she'd decided to tell her mom, but begged her mother not to tell Denise's and Mariah's parents.

Cameron's mom, Anita, listened to her distraught daughter, grateful not only that Cameron didn't participate in the shoplifting but also that she felt safe enough to talk about what happened. Anita wanted to retain her daughter's trust, but she also knew that if it had been Cameron stealing, she would want her daughter to face the consequences and learn that theft causes harm. Anita and Cameron talked for a while about stealing. Cameron wondered if maybe it wasn't so bad to steal from a big store because no one would get hurt, and that's why her friends were doing it, but Anita told Cameron that stealing is wrong no matter how big the store. She also explained that when people shoplift, the prices go up for everyone whether they are rich, poor, or on fixed incomes. She pointed out that stealing hurts the thieves, too, because they lose respect for others and themselves.

Anita came up with an idea that would protect Cameron from backlash, but would still help Denise and Mariah learn about respecting property. She told Cameron that she would like to meet with her homeroom teacher and explain what had happened. She said she would offer to help Cameron's teacher get some materials and information to conduct a lesson on stealing. Cameron thought the idea was pretty good, but made her mother promise not to say who had shoplifted. Anita agreed.

Two weeks later, Cameron came home from school and told her mother what her teacher had done that day. Cameron explained that her teacher had the students describe different ways of stealing, everything from shoplifting to stealing people's ideas (plagiarizing and cheating), to parents lying about their child's age to pay less at a movie, even to insider trading in the stock market. The students had to come up with all the ways in which stealing hurt people. They even talked about whether it was ever okay to steal if you were starving or needed medicine you couldn't afford. The last thing they talked about was what to do if you had taken something that didn't belong to you. They wrote the following list on the board:

- Give it back
- Give it back anonymously if you're afraid you'll get into trouble otherwise
- Give money back if you've used it up (for example, if you stole a candy bar and ate it)
- Give the money to charity if you're scared to give it back to the store
- Decide not to take anything that doesn't belong to you again

When the class was over, Cameron's teacher encouraged the students to give back anything they might have taken, whether from a store, their parents and siblings, or their classmates. She acknowledged that it might be frightening to admit that you'd stolen something, and so she explained that she would put a box in the back of the room for things that anyone might have taken from another classmate. She told the students they could put items in the box anonymously if they wanted to, and invited them to look in the box for things that they had been missing.

A few days later, the teacher began the day by reading a note she had received from a boy in the class. This is what it said:

To whoever took my pen,
I just want to let you know that I'm really glad to have
my pen back. It was my grandfather's fountain pen,
and when he died, it was the only thing I got from all
his stuff. I miss my grandpa a lot. He was really nice to
me, and when I thought I'd lost his pen, I felt really
bad. I wish you hadn't taken my pen, but I'm really
glad you put it in the box.

What this story illustrates is the interplay necessary to bring a value such as respect to life. While Cameron's values about respecting property were intact, the situation still required a community effort. It's not enough for our own child to know that stealing is wrong; she needs a *community* in which stealing is considered wrong, and she also needs to understand that wrongs can be addressed and potentially rectified. Had Anita comforted Cameron but done nothing, Cameron might have felt alone in her values and hopeless about the worth of individual beliefs in the face of peer disregard for honesty and respect. Instead Anita helped her daughter as well as her daughter's friends, teacher, and the whole class by taking an active role in promoting respect. In so doing she not only honored Cameron's virtue, she surrounded her daughter with more virtuous peers. The children in Cameron's class were invited to be courageous and to act with integrity. Their honesty and trustworthiness were cultivated and nurtured.

Other tips for instilling respect during the middle years

- Explain the difference between liking someone and respecting someone. Your child does not need to like everybody, but he does need to show respect to everybody.

- Help your child come up with a list of behaviors and attitudes that do and don't show respect. Here is an example:

SHOWS RESPECT	SHOWS DISRESPECT
Listening	Ignoring
Being polite	Being rude
Asking	Demanding
Thinking about others' feelings	Thinking only about oneself
Speaking calmly	Yelling
Keeping commitments	Forgetting frequently

Once you've come up with a list you can hang it on a wall for your whole family to use as a guideline both in and out of home. Invite everyone in the family to respectfully remind others when they are not showing respect.

- Establish activities for developing respect toward people outside of your community. This may include family volunteering, letter writing on behalf of political prisoners through organizations like Amnesty International, or charitable giving. You can also create family criteria for purchasing products. For instance, you might develop guidelines similar to the ones below:

  ~Buy fair trade products

  ~Avoid products made in sweatshops

  ~Contact companies whose products you like to find out about their policies on human rights

- You can also create routines that demonstrate respect for the earth. For example, you can set up a recycling system for your glass, metal, and paper garbage and make it a habit to save water by turning off the faucet when brushing teeth or by filling the kitchen sink with water to clean the dishes rather than letting the water run. You can have family rules such as keeping lights off when not in use. You can also create family criteria for purchasing products according to environmental standards that might look something like this:

  ~Buy recycled paper whenever possible

  ~Avoid overpackaged and disposable products

~Replace blown incandescent lightbulbs with compact fluorescent lightbulbs

~Avoid getting toxic cleaners and chemicals

~Choose organic foods

- You can make sure that your family shows respect for animals, too. For example, you can have routines in place to provide the attention and exercise your companion animals need, and you can develop family criteria concerning animal welfare for purchasing products, such as this one:

  ~Avoid meat, dairy, and eggs produced in factory farms

  ~Buy cleaning and personal care products not tested on animals

  ~Adopt unwanted companion animals rather than purchase purebreeds

By having family criteria that all of you develop together around these issues, your children can feel part of living with respect for others.

Responsibility

The middle years of childhood are not the time for too many responsibilities. Our children need to be allowed to be children, and it is not until they are adolescents that significant responsibilities ought to be laid upon them. Still, you can begin to introduce responsibilities in small but meaningful ways, paving the way for your child to put on the mantle of responsibility more fully in a few years. Well-chosen responsibilities during the middle years not only lay the foundation for future responsible behavior, they are also empowering. A certain level of responsibility fosters self-esteem, self-discipline, and perseverance. As they grow up during the middle years, children can be responsible for such basics as keeping their room neat, doing their homework, completing selected household chores, writing thank you cards when they receive gifts, practicing a musical instrument, and following house rules (with your help when needed). Learning and practicing these responsibilities will help your children later take on more significant responsibility for actions and choices that affect others. You can add new responsibilities each year that help your child understand that maturity carries duties and is rewarded with more freedoms.

ELEMENT 4: OFFERING POSITIVE CHOICES

During the middle years of childhood you can begin to give your child opportunities to make more meaningful decisions that put humane values into practice. In our humane education programs, one of the ways in which we teach about and provide options is through Choices Cards. Every card has two similar activities or products printed on each side. For example, we have a card that reads "Keeping all your allowance" on one side and "Giving 10% of your allowance to charity" on the other. Another card reads "Paper napkin" on one side and "Cloth napkin" on the other. Some other cards say "Rugmart Rug" or "Conventional Rug," "Cirque de Soleil" or "Ringling Bros. Circus," "Tofu Pup" or "Hot Dog."

We ask students to consider each card and then to determine which of the two choices harms less and helps more. Often they haven't heard of something on a card, like Rugmart (a label that ensures that a rug was not made by slave labor) or Cirque de Soleil (a circus troupe that does not use animals in their performances). Sometimes a choice is unusual, and students don't know quite what to make of it (like a Tofu Pup) until a member of the class says she's tried one and it's good. The students read each card and analyze the choice in terms of human health and well-being, animal suffering, environmental issues, and any related concerns. The choice is not always clear-cut, nor do the cards reflect the entire range of choices we have, but this activity invites students to consider normative behaviors as well as options that might be more beneficial both to themselves and to others.

Using Choices Cards at home would be contrived, but you can still offer your children choices and explore decisions similar to those presented on the Choices Cards. At dinner you can bring up choices for discussion and ask your children's opinions. You can share real life quandaries and engage your children in debate. One family I know raises questions for discussion at the dinner table fairly often, and they make family decisions about ethical issues, balancing financial constraints and practicality against their wish to make kind choices. For example, at the beginning of the school year when everyone wanted new clothes, the dad brought up the issue of sweatshop labor, resource use, and pollution. The conversation was quite lively. Ten-year-old Rebecca said it was far more important that they make sure that they bought clothes that were produced fairly, and stated she was happy to shop at thrift shops, while Alison, at fourteen, said she couldn't find the right clothes or shoes at the thrift shop in town and hated feeling like her clothes looked stupid. Their dad asked, "How can we make the best decision?" Alison said that there were some better thrift shops in the city, which was an hour and a half away, and her dad asked whether driving all the way to the city would pay off in a greater benefit or not. They came up with a plan to make the trip really worthwhile by getting lots of things done in the city that they'd been putting off. The whole family was involved in the decision-making, and everyone became excited about the trip. Rebecca and Alison were invited to put their kindness into effect in a practical way and to show their compassion through their clothing choices. Their parents helped them practice the quality of choosing wisely.

Learning that choices exist to improve the world and put humane values into practice is very empowering to children, especially during the middle years when their developing consciences demand fairness and justice. By offering and discussing choices in your home, you will help your child move from liking the good to doing the good. Make sure, however, that you don't impose all *your* choices on your children. It's important that your child feels that she can make some decisions that come from her values rather than solely from yours. This can be difficult if you hold your values very dear and you don't want to see your child making different choices than you, but in order for your child to ultimately *be* humane, she needs to be allowed to make some of her own decisions rather than simply follow yours.

WHAT TO DO WHEN YOUR NINE-YEAR-OLD DAUGHTER BEGS YOU TO LET HER GO TO A PG-13 MOVIE THAT MOST OF HER FRIENDS ARE SEEING

a) Give yourself time to respond

Let your daughter know you will think about it and get back to her. Explain that you don't want to make a snap decision without more information and thought.

b) Elements 1 and 2: Gather information and think critically

Go see the movie yourself, perhaps with your spouse and/or some other parents of girls your daughter's age. Watch the film with a critical eye and discuss the content and message among yourselves. Think about the possible effects on your daughter. Consider what qualities the film promotes.

c) Element 3: Use the three Rs

Ask yourself whether the film will impact your daughter's reverence, respectfulness, and sense of responsibility in positive or negative ways, or whether it will have no obvious impact either way.

d) Element 4: Make a positive choice

Whatever your decision, explain why you made the choice you did. If you allow her to see the film, let her know that you did so only after watching the film yourself, thinking about it, and considering its impact on her mind, heart, and soul. If there are aspects of the film that you want to explore with her after she's seen it, bring those up so that you can promote the three Rs and possibly analyze parts of the film critically together.

If you choose not to allow your daughter to see the film, share the process by which you came to that decision so that your daughter knows that you were always thinking about what was best for her rather than relying upon an arbitrary rule or immediate reaction.

e) Stay flexible and be prepared to revisit the issue

The choice you make in one instance won't necessarily apply to another. You may not always need to see every film to make a decision if you've heard from respected sources that a certain film does or does not have content that you feel is appropriate.

SCHOOL

Since school has such an enormous influence on your children, it's worth thinking carefully about their schooling if you want to instill your values and raise them to be humane. Some families will have a choice about where to send their children to school. Well-to-do people can choose to live in a district with a good public school, or they can consider private schools to find the best fit for their children; however, most families have no choice but to send their children to the local public school, regardless of whether or not it best meets their children's needs. Some parents will choose to homeschool their child rather than rely upon the local school, but this choice also requires resources that not all parents have available to them. Whether or not you have the opportunity to send your child to the school of your choice, though you still have the power to influence your child's education and to work to make sure that your deepest values are supported, or at least not undermined, at school. An in-depth discussion of education reform is beyond the scope of this book, but there are steps that you can take as a parent to help ensure that your child's school supports humane values. If most people subscribe to the list of best qualities of human beings listed in Chapter 1, then we have the power to make those qualities the foundation of our schools.

HOW TO BE A POSITIVE FORCE IN YOUR CHILD'S SCHOOL

The suggestions below apply to both elementary and secondary schools:

- Join the PTA (Parent-Teacher Association) and help move the school toward the values you cherish.
- If at all possible, volunteer during school hours and form a partnership with your child's teachers so that you are helping them even as you encourage them to meet the needs of your child. Make sure that you are an ally of the school and the teachers rather than a critical adversary; otherwise your volunteer efforts may hinder rather than help both the school and your child.
- Organize a group of parents and sympathetic teachers and administrators and create a Humane School Charter toward which to strive. Make certain that you come up with an ideal that reflects many voices. The Humane

School Charter might include expectations around student and teacher behaviors as well as goals for a greener school through recycling, environmental and humane pest management, compact fluorescent lighting, etc. The Charter can also include goals for the cafeteria so that foods are healthy and humane, and for the school's relationship to animals, including a policy about classroom animals and dissection to ensure that the school does not participate in the suffering of animals. Once the Charter is complete, distribute it to the school community and invite volunteer involvement to help put it into practice.

- Fight the corporate takeover of school curricula. If your child's school is using lesson plans provided free by corporations such as Exxon, DuPont, Proctor and Gamble, Pizza Hut, McDonald's, or some other company, discuss your concerns about corporate curricula with your child's teachers and administrators. More and more industry-produced curricula are finding their way into cash-strapped schools. This takeover of education by multinational corporations represents a real threat to critical thinking, honest information, the health of our children, and the availability of humane choices in school. Unless teachers are using these curricula as materials for a lesson on critical thinking, the Exxon curriculum that suggests to children that Exxon left Prince William Sound better than before its oil spill, or the Beef Board's lesson that teaches kids to eat beef unless they want to grow up to be small, or the Proctor and Gamble materials that teach children that disposable diapers are better for the environment than cloth become merely veiled advertisements endorsed by the school.

- Research resources for schools. Many nonprofit organizations offer speakers free of charge to schools, and their presentations can introduce children to a range of issues, concerns, and solutions to problems. Make sure that you are providing teachers with a variety of viewpoints so the children will have opportunities for critical thinking.

- Support and promote the humane education movement. When all schools have humane educators on the faculty and humane education is integrated into the curricula, it will be much easier to raise humane children because humane values will be reinforced at school. Teachers can get humane education materials and training so that they are better able to offer humane education to their students.

SIX

ADOLESCENCE (THE TEENAGE YEARS)

A growing number of youngsters are profoundly disillusioned by the ailing planet they
inherited. They span the continuum from idealistic young people to those who ... have little
faith in traditional institutions. What they share
is a yearning for a just world without the artificial distinctions that impede all beings from
fulfilling their destinies in peace.

— ED DUVIN

ADOLESCENCE CAN BE A TIME of deep idealism and positive choices. It can also be a time of weakening family relationships, foolhardy decisions, sexual promiscuity, drugs, alcohol, and tobacco abuse, and other unhealthy behaviors and rebellions. Whether our teenagers enter a time of healthy growth and development or succumb to peer pressures and destructive behaviors has much to do with us. If we are willing to become their ally rather than their adversary in negotiating the rocky terrain of emerging adulthood, and do so with an open mind and an open heart, they will know that they can trust us as they explore their path and gradually move away from our protective arms.

As a humane educator, I enjoy teaching teenagers more than students of any other age. I love their energy and passion, their skepticism and commitment to truth, their emerging self-discoveries and eagerness to alternately play devil's advocate and dive into what they believe. I also feel immense compassion for their vulnerability, their fears, their confusion, their unmet desires, their yearning to be grown up and free, the isolation many feel from their parents, and, often, their doubt and despair. I remember these emotions well. While adolescence can try everyone's patience (most of all that of the teenagers themselves), it is a profound developmental transition that deserves to be honored, not simply endured. Our adolescent children need us to hold them in the highest esteem, to believe in their capacity to emerge from this period in their lives whole and triumphant. If we can let go of our expectations and hopes that our adolescent children will fulfill our own dreams, we can focus on a goal that is, I believe, more important than any other: that our children emerge into adulthood as humane people who know how to take responsibility for themselves and their world.

THE CHALLENGES OF ADOLESCENCE

Our adolescent children are exposed to many images and role models that are dangerous — psychologically, spiritually, and physically. From anorexic models to violent characters in movies, from "cool" actors smoking in films to cynicism presented as chic, there is much our teenagers have to negotiate. They are tempted by consumerism and greed, and they face a maze of competing influences and messages that beckon them to abandon the path toward becoming deeply humane. For example, consider the following: a 2002 National Public Radio segment featured a report about Hot Topic, a chain of stores in malls that cater to teenagers. Since adolescents often congregate in malls, Hot Topic filled the niche for a 'cool' chain of stores to attract them. The stores play the latest music, send their young employees to concerts to scope out what's hip, and turn products around quickly to meet fads and trends. Betsy McLaughlin, the chain's CEO, said to NPR reporter Susan Stone, "We are trying to emulate what's going on in a teenager's head. And that's one of the reasons why we feel that a new product every day is in line with a teenager's attention span." Retail analyst Joe Techlitz asserts, "When you're fifteen years old, there's really no other way to build an identity than the clothing that you wear and maybe the music that you listen to."

It is discouraging to think that corporations and their CEOs perceive adolescents to be mere targets for their skilled manipulation in the marketplace, and that they prey on teenagers' desire to find an identity for themselves by selling them products. It is more than cynical to think that an adolescent's identity can only be created through clothing and musical tastes. Such attitudes are profoundly damaging both to teenagers themselves and to our world, which needs its youth to be awake, aware, and committed to discovering who they are beyond their appearance. Hot Topic is just one of many examples of the ways in which our culture holds adolescents in poor regard, expects them to be shallow, and attempts to use them to make a profit. All the more reason to commit ourselves as parents to nurturing humane values in our adolescents. It is humane values, and the lives flowing from them, that will give our children rich and meaningful identities that do not demand a new CD or T-shirt each day to be sustained.

The challenges our adolescent children face differ, based on gender, class, sexual orientation, region, and environment. Inner city boys are faced with violence that is largely absent from the lives of prep school kids (who may more frequently consider suicide as an escape from pressures and expectations that for some are too overwhelming to bear). Rural and suburban teens have a greater risk of being involved in drug- and alcohol- related car accidents. Most homosexual teens still have to choose between the soul-destroying closet and the hatred they will likely face if they are open about their sexual orientation. Wherever you live, whatever gender your children are, and whatever your economic situation, your teenager will confront certain challenges — and the more you understand the specific circumstances your teens face, the more you can effectively help them.

THE CHALLENGES BOYS FACE

Compare the images of strong, powerful men today with the images from thirty, forty, or fifty years ago. The original Superman looks flabby compared to Christopher Reeve in the 1980s, and Christopher Reeve's Superman looks almost weak compared to Sylvester Stallone as Rambo or Arnold Schwarzenegger as the Terminator. (Even G.I. Joe has bulked up in recent years, as have virtually all children's action figures, offering our young sons ever more unrealistic ideals to emulate.)

And it isn't simply male bodies that have changed. Guns are bigger; violence is more graphic. Power is less often identified with strength of character, compassion, and wisdom (which were significant, defining qualities of the old superheroes) and instead has become synonymous with deadly weapons, wealth, and the capacity to dominate rather than help others. Boys are faced with both impossible and tragic images of manhood. Empathy and care are often considered weak, especially by the boys and men who are the most disenfranchised in our society. But it is not simply the disenfranchised who perceive compassion as weak. Most

Fortune 500 CEOs (the vast majority of whom are men) know that if they place people over profits or compassion over competition, their fall from their positions of leadership and financial success will likely be swift and unforgiving. To genuinely feel compassion for their factory workers in Indonesia or Mexico would necessitate ensuring them a living wage and decent working conditions, a choice that could diminish profits. It is the unusual CEO who tries to change this system, to forgo a multi-million-dollar salary in favor of a low six-figure income for the sake of greater equity and fairness, or to guide production toward ecologically sustainable and safe practices and products. By and large, these men have been acculturated to dominate and succeed at the expense of others rather than through cooperation and humane decision-making.

Men in our society, whether they are elevated to the highest status or eek out an existence in poverty, are often taught implicitly to repress their emotions (with the notable exception of anger). If being humane includes such virtues as compassion, kindness, and generosity, and if expressing these feelings and attitudes demonstrates weakness, puts one in danger, or results in a fall from grace that seems irrevocable, then our sons face enormous obstacles in being humane.

Boys also face a dearth of good role models. For every compassionate star athlete there are dozens of others fighting each other in brawls on the field, ice, or court. For every Patch Adams, there are scores of Rambo look-alikes in the movies. For every Will Hunting who finds a strong, empathic therapist, there are thousands of adolescent boys who are offered little help. For every young male hero who succeeds by virtue of his character, there are hundreds who appear to succeed on their physical prowess, their ability to dominate others, or their success at seducing women. The many boys who have little or no contact with their fathers, or whose fathers do not model humane values may be even more susceptible to media images unless they have found good male role models elsewhere.

THE CHALLENGES GIRLS FACE

While girls today have more varied role models than their grand-mothers did and are invited to pursue their own interests and talents, their success is often defined by attributes that have nothing to do with their character, their talents, or their intellect. Although girls have career choices and opportunities to learn and succeed in most of the same arenas as boys, they are still at the mercy of cultural imperatives that valorize superficial qualities. Advertising will teach our daughters that their bodies need to be fixed, and this lesson will accompany them well into their older years (when our wrinkles and gray hair will not lend us status but will instead be problems to be solved through youth-enhancing products). They will learn that so many parts of themselves should be changed. Their body hair should be removed while the hair on their head should be properly coifed. Their faces should be covered in make-up, and their weight should be reduced. Ads for feminine deodorant sprays and douches will teach them that their genitals are disgusting, and they will be forever wondering if they smell bad. Chances are that their breasts will not fit the cultural standard either. One print ad for a hair product placed in teen magazines reads: "Your breasts may be too big, too saggy, too pert, too far apart, too close together, too A-cup, too lopsided, too padded, too pointy, too pendulous, or two mosquito bites. But with Dep styling products, at least you can have your hair the way you want it."

Girls often emerge from the middle years of childhood with their self-esteem intact, and their love of life vital. Then adolescence descends, and many find themselves dieting, bingeing, spending their days focused on make-up and clothes, trying to meet a standard that is impossible to achieve. Their self-worth may disintegrate before your very eyes. Whereas they may have once loved to learn, in adolescence they may be barely able to focus on their studies; whereas they may have once loved sports, they may now self-consciously reject the strong bodies that used to give them such pleasure and freedom.

Some girls try very hard to remain intact. I know an adolescent girl named Sara who rejected many of the messages she received from the culture. She was capable and attractive and had close friends. She also had a devoted boyfriend. But she didn't shave her legs, her bikini line or her armpits. One day her mother told her that her body hair was disgusting and offensive. Sara laughed. She asked her mother if she found John's hair disgusting, too (John was her older brother). Her mother responded, "Of course not." "So, the hair that grows naturally on John's body is okay, but the hair that grows naturally on mine isn't?" Sara asked. Her mother snorted and said that she just couldn't talk to Sara. This story might have illustrated tremendous strength of will and self-confidence, but the truth is that Sara had managed to defy a social norm and feel good about herself *until* her mother told her that her body hair was disgusting. She knew that her hairy legs and unshaved bikini line and armpits were out of the ordinary, but she had felt good when she stopped shaving. She felt that she was taking her body back from the culture that would have her manipulate it for other people's sake, and she had never felt disgusting until her mother told her she was. This damage to her body image made her all the more susceptible to shallow messages, and she became increasingly self-conscious and self-absorbed, which in turn led her further away from healthy and humane choice-making on behalf of either herself or others.

If girls focus their time and energy on their physical appearance, they will inevitably be neglecting the development of their own spirits, passions, and capacities. While many boys face challenges to becoming compassionate, generous, and caring, many girls face challenges to their self-respect and integrity.

None of these descriptions of gender challenges is meant to imply that boys don't face problems of self-respect or that girls don't confront obstacles to being compassionate. I have written in generalities because, unfortunately, these stereotyped challenges still exist. Recognizing them, even though they do not necessarily apply fully to our own children, can help us to better parent our adolescent sons and daughters.

FACING THE CHALLENGES

During adolescence, it may appear that our children want nothing to do with us. They may talk to their friends for hours, but have little to say to us. They may become secretive and pull back from interactions. It's important not to acquiesce in this distancing by pulling away ourselves or ignoring our teenage children. They need us as much during adolescence as they needed us as toddlers. In fact, they may need us more than ever. There may never be a time in our children's lives when their paths are as difficult as they are in adolescence. As our sons and daughters become adolescents, we will not be able to control the images and messages they receive. Their peer group and mainstream culture will become even more influential. This is all the more reason to become adept at using the Four Elements. The Four Elements will provide the tools to help your teenagers negotiate adolescence successfully and enable them to emerge whole and humane from this challenging period in their lives. The following stories illustrate how parents can use the different elements with their children.

ELEMENTS 1 AND 2: PROVIDING INFORMATION AND CULTIVATING CRITICAL THINKING

BRIAN, CHARLENE AND BILL

Brian was sixteen when his parents, Charlene and Bill, became concerned that he was spending more and more time on the Internet, was uninterested in interacting with them or his younger siblings, and seemed to be becoming isolated. Brian didn't seem unhappy. In fact, he seemed strangely energized, but nonetheless, Bill and Charlene felt that something was wrong. One day when Brian was at school, Charlene, a social worker, happened to be home for a couple of hours. She decided to look on Brian's computer to find out what he was doing for hours each night. Although she was uncomfortable with invading Brian's privacy, all of her efforts at communicating with him in recent months had failed, and she felt she had to do something.

Charlene discovered that Brian was involved with a new religion that looked to her like a cult. He was corresponding with a charismatic spiritual leader and several devotees, all of whom were urging Brian to join their community. Some of the advice they were giving Brian was actually good. They were telling him to seek truth from within, to meditate each day, to eat healthy foods, and to abstain from sex or drugs. But they were also encouraging Brian to reject his parents' and teachers' values and to view the world as an illusion that he could escape through spirituality, and specifically through becoming a devotee in their particular sect.

That night, Bill and Charlene talked about what they should do. They were not religious people themselves and had never taken their children to church. Clearly, Brian wanted something that he was not getting at home or within his own culture, but Bill and Charlene were not convinced that what Brian had found was good for him. They considered their options. They could forbid Brian to communicate with the religious leader and his followers (which probably wouldn't work). Since Brian was essentially healthy, they could ignore the situation (which they felt was dangerous), or they could find out more themselves and explore spiritual questions with their son. They chose the last option.

The next night, Bill and Charlene told Brian they wanted to talk to him. Charlene admitted to Brian that she had learned about his involvement with the religious group by reading his emails, and explained that she had been very worried about him and felt she had to violate his privacy in order to be a responsible parent. Brian was furious. Charlene and Bill let him vent his anger, steering clear of being confrontational. In fact, Charlene confessed that she felt terrible about sneaking into his private correspondence, and she apologized. But both Charlene and Bill insisted that it was their job as Brian's parents to make sure that they protected him from anything, including a religious group, that could potentially harm him, and they told him that they were concerned about the religious leader and some of his opinions. Then they told Brian that they wanted to learn more about the religion he'd discovered and suggested that all three of them attend a talk by the spiritual leader at his temple, which was an hour away.

Brian was shocked. He had been unable to attend the meetings or talks at the temple because he didn't have any way to get there and had been too scared to ask his parents if he could go. Their willingness to actually visit the temple came as a complete surprise. He didn't really want his parents to visit the temple with him, though. He was afraid that they would embarrass him or make critical comments. Charlene and Bill could see that Brian was struggling with the thought of his parents accompanying him, and Bill said, "Brian, we promise that we'll be respectful at the temple, and we won't embarrass you, okay?"

The next weekend they all went to the temple. Brian met the spiritual leader whom he had admired so much, and introduced his parents. The family listened to the talk that day. It was about non-attachment. The spiritual leader urged the devotees to let go of their attachments to possessions, to thoughts, and to feelings, and to find a peaceful center. He helped the attendees recognize the ways in which their minds would scurry from one thought or desire to another and led them in a meditation to detach from these thoughts and feelings and to simply observe them.

Afterwards, the family joined the community for lunch and talked to the devotees who lived at the temple. Bill and Charlene asked them questions about their daily lives and about their hopes for the future. Most of them didn't have any future plans. They were happy to serve their spiritual master and to do what he told them. They said they were trying to live fully in the present rather than focus on the future and had renounced their worldly attachments. Brian just listened.

When they left the temple, Brian asked his parents what they thought. It was the first time in months that Brian had seemed to care about his parents' opinions. Charlene and Bill told Brian what they liked about the meditation and the talk, as well as what concerned them. Then they asked Brian questions about what he thought, and whether the life of a devotee appealed to him. They wanted to know if it helped Brian to meditate. They asked him about his beliefs. Brian shared so much with his parents that day. He explained that he wasn't convinced that the physical world was an illusion, but that he felt much better since he'd started meditating. He said that most of his friends at school were into really stupid stuff, but that the temple was teaching about important things that made sense to him. He admitted that he thought he wanted to join the community before going to the temple, but listening to the devotees talk about their lives wasn't as great as he'd thought. He wasn't sure.

Bill and Charlene told Brian that they were interested in reading more and talking to Brian about his spiritual practice, and offered to take him to the temple again if he wanted. They suggested that the three of them try the daily meditation and read one of the temple books and then talk about it each week. That night, Brian hugged his parents for the first time in months and told them he loved them. Just before he went to bed he said, "I didn't think you'd understand. Thanks."

By the end of the year, Brian was not involved with that particular temple, but he still maintained a meditation practice, as did Bill. The whole family actually visited several alternative spiritual communities as well as a few traditional religious institutions. Brian's interest in religion had turned into an exploration of spirituality and values, and the whole family had learned a lot together.

What would have happened had Brian's parents tried to squelch his emerging interest in spirituality? What would have happened had they tried to forbid Brian from becoming involved with a religious community that they didn't approve of? What would have happened had they ignored the situation altogether? Chances are they either would have alienated their son or left him without the skills to properly assess the religious teachings. Instead, supportive involvement helped everyone to grow, and Brian negotiated a potentially dangerous period in his adolescence emerging more educated and wise in the process. Although Bill and Charlene did not initiate the exploration of spirituality, they went on the journey with their son, gathering information together and bringing critical thinking into the discussion.

KATHERINE AND FRAN

My friend Fran was concerned about her daughter, Katherine. Just before her fourteenth birthday, Katherine (who had turned into a beautiful young woman almost overnight) asked Fran for a subscription to a teen fashion magazine. Fran was worried that Katherine would fall prey to the skewed priorities she would discover in such a magazine and might focus all her energies on her looks rather than her character and abilities.

Katherine had never been a particularly good student. Although she was quite bright, she suffered from a reading disability that made it difficult to keep up with her peers in class. When she entered adolescence, Katherine discovered that her beauty gained her more attention, praise, and popularity than any of her other skills.

Fran told Katherine she would get her the subscription to the magazine, but only if Katherine agreed that they would spend some time looking at the magazine together when each issue arrived. Katherine thought it was a little strange that her mother wanted to read a teen magazine with her, but said okay.

When the first issue came, Fran sat down with Katherine and looked at it with her. They read some articles, completed a quiz titled, "How to keep your guy," and looked at the fashion spread. They were laughing together about some of the articles, and Fran asked Katherine questions about what she liked and why. The conversation was comfortable and good, and Katherine enjoyed her mother's attention, especially because her mom seemed open and not critical of her. In fact, Katherine felt that her mom really wanted to know about what was important to her. She even admitted to her mother that she wished she were as thin as the models in the magazine and told her about an anorexic girl in her high school whom she secretly admired.

Fran knew that she was in dangerous territory. She didn't want to start lecturing her daughter about anorexia or criticize her daughter's obsession with appearances, but she knew she couldn't remain silent if her daughter descended into unhealthy habits and behaviors. She decided to try a different approach. She asked her daughter questions about how it might feel to be one of those models, about what might happen to models when they turned thirty, about what it would be like to be forever dieting, and about the relationships the models might have with other women and men.

At first Katherine talked about how great it must be to be rich and famous and adored, but then she paused for a moment. In a quieter voice she said that she wondered if the models could really trust anyone: "It must be hard not knowing whether someone wants to be with you because you're beautiful, or because they actually like you." Fran asked Katherine if she ever felt like that. "Sometimes," she said. "A lot of guys want to go out with me these days, but I don't really know if it's just because of how I look. And now the popular girls want to hang out with me, too."

As the months went by, Fran was able to help Katherine think about the ways in which the magazine articles and the advertisements manipulated girls, and she helped Katherine to analyze the ads and understand their hidden messages. Fran was careful not to simply criticize the magazine, but rather to invite Katherine to become aware of how the magazine might influence and affect girls. Katherine actually began to become critical of the magazine herself and eventually brought ads to the dinner table to talk about them. "Look at this!" she said to Fran as she held up a Calvin Klein ad for jeans. "This girl is about twelve and she's practically naked with this guy leaning over her like he's in control of her or something!" As Katherine began to recognize the ways in which companies were trying to manipulate her, she started to rebel against the messages in the magazine. She lost interest in conforming to the images she was seeing and began to enjoy the power she felt when she could accurately identify the ways in which corporations were targeting her to consume their products. She made some new friends at school who were more interested in social issues than appearances, and when these girls told her about companies using sweatshop labor, Katherine joined their after-school club, which was working to ensure that the school's athletic uniforms weren't made in sweatshops.

Not only did Katherine avoid the trap into which many physically beautiful girls can fall, she also discovered ideals that were important to her and found a path that didn't rely on her physical attributes, a path that enabled her to feel proud of herself.

Like Bill and Charlene, Fran found a way to bring information and critical thinking into her teenager's life without alienating her daughter. She was able to both connect with and guide her daughter by staying involved and supportive, while helping Katherine move through a difficult period. She neither abandoned her daughter to advertising agencies nor tried to control her daughter's values. Instead, she brought her attention to the problem that her daughter faced, offered herself as a nonjudgmental guide and teacher, and trusted her daughter's ability to rely upon the power of her intellect rather than fall victim to the power of her insecurities. She offered Katherine the skills to gather information and think deeply and critically. Katherine emerged from this period compassionate, wise beyond her years, more generous, and committed to learning and thinking about the world around her.

ADAM AND RICHARD

Adam grew six inches the summer he turned sixteen. His body filled out, hair started growing on his chin, and he got his driver's license. Adam's father, Richard, was anxious. Adam had always been a kind and well-behaved boy, and Richard had hardly ever worried about him, but suddenly what had once seemed like such a blessing — Adam's goodness and obedient nature — became a potential threat. Adam was a follower, and Richard was concerned about who and what Adam might follow. Although Adam had good friends whom he'd known since grade school, his high school had a reputation for drug use, and Richard could see that Adam had suddenly become somewhat taken with the drug-using crowd at school. He was watching a lot of MTV, had recently adopted a swagger, and was testing the waters to see if he could swim in the new world of more wayward teens. Richard knew he'd raised Adam with healthy values, but would these values remain intact in the face of adolescent peer pressures?

Richard sat down with Adam and asked him some hard questions. "What are you going to do when you're driving some night and your buddies pass you a joint or a bottle of beer? What are you going to say?" Richard really pushed Adam to answer, mimicking the kind of pressure he might have to endure. "What will you say when they call you a coward, Adam? What are you going to do when they light up in the car? Are you going to follow the crowd even if it's stupid and dangerous?"

Adam was taken aback. He'd never seen his dad act this way. He didn't really know what he would do. He'd barely hung out with the kind of kids his father was describing, but in fact, those were just the kind of guys he was starting to meet and like at school. They seemed cool, and he wanted to be cool, too.

Richard said, "I know I'm being hard on you, Adam, but that's what's going to happen, and you need to be prepared. You're sixteen now, and you've got to know how to make good decisions." Then Richard shared a story from his own adolescence. He described the night of his senior prom thirty years earlier. Richard told Adam about his best friend, Jack, a star athlete with a scholarship to the state university. Jack and Louise (Jack's girlfriend and the prom queen) had been drinking throughout the night. "Jack thought nothing bad could happen to him," Richard told his son. "He acted like he was invulnerable and life was a huge adventure. He didn't think twice about getting behind the wheel. Ten minutes after they left the prom, Jack crashed his car, and Louise was killed."

Over the next several weeks Richard took Adam to an Alcoholics Anonymous and a Narcotics Anonymous meeting so that Adam could hear the stories of people whose lives were damaged by addiction, and he introduced Adam to Mrs. Rand, Louise's mother, who was now seventy-four years old and actively involved in MADD (Mothers Against Drunk Driving). Adam felt awkward at AA and NA and was uncomfortable meeting Mrs. Rand, but he found the meetings really eye-opening and was honored that his dad thought he was mature enough to hear these stories. He felt prepared to face some of the pressures at school and didn't think that it was quite as cool to use drugs or drink.

The scenario that his father had acted out with him eventually happened, almost exactly like his father predicted. He was leaving a party one night, and several classmates asked him if he'd drive them home. The guy they'd come to the party with was passed out on the couch, and they needed a ride. Adam said sure, but when he was driving, they offered him a joint. Adam said, "No thanks." "You scared, man? I don't think I've ever seen you take a hit, Adam. Come on, try it." Adam *was* scared. He was scared of smoking dope, especially while he was driving, but he realized that his bigger fear was that he would be considered uncool. He searched inside for courage, felt his heart pounding, and answered, as calmly as he could, "I don't smoke, guys. Quit asking." Despite his fear, Adam's voice held conviction, and the boys left him alone after that.

Richard had had an easy time raising Adam. For sixteen years, he'd never had any major conflicts with his son. Adam was a gentle boy, well-liked and well-behaved. It would have been simple enough to be oblivious to the danger that threatened Adam when he turned sixteen, but Richard was not complacent. He remained alert and involved, and his guidance may have averted his son's potential drug use. By taking Adam to AA and NA meetings, he offered his son information that balanced the allure of drugs and alcohol presented by the users at school. By introducing Adam to Mrs. Rand, he gave his son the chance to learn about the tragedies that befall people who drink and drive. Through his dad's questioning and "field trips" Adam learned how to think critically about drugs and alcohol. In the end, Adam found courage and will that he hadn't even known he possessed.

In these three stories, all the parents recognized that their teenagers needed information and help to think critically. They realized that their adolescents were no longer children and that they couldn't control their actions by simply saying no. They needed to become involved as guides and allies. In each of these situations, however, it would have been easier for the parents to ignore the problem. Charlene and Bill could have avoided a conflict with Brian and instead periodically monitored his email behind his back. Fran could have simply bought Katherine a subscription to the teen magazine without involving herself further. Richard could certainly have dismissed his worries about Adam since Adam was such a good kid. But these parents didn't take the easy route; they chose to get *more* involved with their children and to actively bring information and critical thinking to the situation their adolescent faced. By doing so they not only may have averted much more significant problems down the road, but they also became closer to their teenagers.

Clearly, I have shared success stories, and I know that the outcomes of our individual struggles with our teens won't always be so perfect. It's my hope, however, that these stories will inspire you to use the first two of the Four Elements when you are confronted with a problem, a challenge, or even a small concern regarding your teenager.

During adolescence, providing information and teaching critical thinking can't be done according to a textbook formula, but rather must unfold as the interests or needs of the teenager become more defined. If there is information that you want your adolescent to have, like Richard wanted Adam to have about drugs and alcohol, you can find meaningful ways to share this information with your son or daughter, utilizing the resources in your community to help. Fran wanted her daughter to become a critical thinker so that she would not fall victim to destructive cultural messages, and so she helped her daughter not by preventing the messages from entering their home, but by teaching her daughter how to analyze and understand those messages. Bill and Charlene didn't crush their son's spiritual impulses, but they taught him how to remain clear-headed as he explored a religious path.

What information do you think *your* adolescent needs? Does he need information and skills to solve problems without fighting and violence? Do you want her to know how to earn and manage money? Is your adolescent in a peer group that endangers her values? Is he particularly susceptible to media images or prone to emulating actors with values opposed to your own? Does your child need more information in order to make humane choices on behalf of other people, other species, or the environment?

As you identify the areas in which your adolescent could use information and guidance, you can look for opportunities to share this information. Rather than set yourself up solely as the teacher, you can become a student alongside your teenager, asking questions, listening as much as you speak, and seeking out others from whom you can both learn.

As you reflect upon the stories above, ask yourself what qualities these teenagers and their parents manifested. What qualities did they cultivate and honor? Brian's parents supported their son's curiosity and efforts to seek wisdom and truth and helped him to develop his capacity to learn and think. Katherine learned to be vigilant in her critique of cultural messages and became more compassionate toward others. Richard helped Adam to become more courageous in his own convictions and to find self-confidence in his own values. All of these adolescents became more humane because they were embodying more of the best qualities of human beings.

ELEMENT 3: INSTILLING THE THREE Rs

Adolescence can be quite a self-absorbed time, and insecurities actually foster more self-absorption. In a vicious cycle, self-absorption can then foster more insecurities. Opportunities to reach outside of one's inner life and turmoil, to connect with and help others, and to act upon concerns outside of oneself help our adolescents gain maturity, build self-esteem and move towards healthy and responsible adulthood.

How can you nurture your teenagers' compassion and reverence for the good and instill their respect for others? How can you help them become more responsible? You will most likely be unsuccessful if you say to your daughter, "Can't you think about anyone other than yourself?" or demand that your son volunteer at the local nursing home, but if you pay attention to your teenagers' interests and concerns, stay alert for opportunities to inspire reverence, respect, and responsibility, and encourage them to act upon their concerns, you may be able to guide them toward the fulfillment of the three Rs. For example, if you notice that your fourteen-year-old daughter loves animals, you might take her to a wildlife rehabilitation center or an animal shelter and suggest that she inquire about volunteer opportunities, or even part-time paid positions. If your son expresses concerns about the environment and you hear about a river clean up in your town, you can suggest that your family participate. Initial groans of protest will likely be replaced with strong feelings of accomplishment by the end of the day.

There are many community opportunities to learn about what is happening both regionally and around the world that also provide information about what people can do to make a difference. Places of worship periodically host educational events and fundraisers, and nonprofit organizations frequently bring issues and information to the community. You can invite your adolescent children to join you at these events. Often at such talks and films the audience's reverence and empathy are awakened, their respect for others grows, and they become more empowered to act responsibly for the sake of others. Compassion, ignited by new information, can then turn into action.

Compassion in action is the realization of the three Rs. Fully manifested, the three Rs bring us back to what is truly important in life: the love we can share with others, the ways in which generosity and kindness can heal suffering and transform us, and the development of our souls. Most teenagers desperately need to feel of use in this world. They know that they are too old to act like self-centered children, but they are also too young to find much more than tedious work at McDonald's. Their hearts are often crying out for more opportunities to contribute and be responsible citizens. The world also needs young people. They have energy, passion, and vitality to offer to those who welcome their gifts. When young people care, when their compassion is engaged, they become a force that is extraordinarily powerful.

In the story that follows you will see how one family confronted the challenges of their self-absorbed daughter and helped nurture the three Rs.

MIRIAM, ABE AND RACHEL

Miriam and Abe's sixteen-year-old daughter, Rachel, was short-tempered and rude to both them and her younger siblings. She had become completely self-centered and almost impossible to live with. At their wits end, Miriam and Abe consulted their rabbi, who gave them some advice. He recommended that they make the suffering of others real to Rachel in order to awaken her concern for people other than herself. The rabbi, who had known Rachel her whole life, reminded Miriam and Abe that Rachel had always been motivated by the concept of fairness. "She's strong-willed and determined, and if you can help her direct her energy toward something positive, I believe she will do great things," the rabbi told them. He suggested that Miriam and Abe start renting movies that depicted heroes who fought against injustice, and then he recommended some titles, including *Gandhi*, *Sarafini*, *Erin Brokovich*, *Silkwood*, and *Norma Rae*. "Tell Rachel that she's welcome to join you once she's finished her homework," the rabbi said. Then he added, "And once Rachel starts to care about others, give her something to do with her passion. Let her help make a difference."

None of Rachel's younger siblings were permitted to watch these videos because of the adult content in the films, but Miriam and Abe told Rachel that they believed she was old enough and could watch them if she wanted. Rachel did watch the videos with her parents, and afterwards they talked about the themes and messages and about the incredible women and men who fought for justice. Rachel came alive in these discussions. She was deeply moved by some of the movies and very vocal about her opinions. Miriam and Abe led the discussion toward issues that affected people in their own community, and then began collecting newspaper articles about a situation in a nearby poor, predominantly minority neighborhood in which a waste disposal company was trying to build an incinerator. The incinerator threatened to expose the neighborhood to high levels of toxins. Rachel was incensed when she heard about these plans and asked her parents what she could do to stop them. Miriam suggested that Rachel write a letter to the local paper. Rachel liked the idea of having her opinion in print, and she drafted a compelling letter. It was published the following week. June, an African-American senior at her school (whom Rachel had known only in passing), told Rachel she had seen her letter and was really glad that she had written it. She also let Rachel know about a neighborhood effort to stop the incinerator and invited her to help. Rachel said she would. Pretty soon Rachel was spending most of her afternoons and weekends working with June on the campaign to stop the incinerator.

Rachel was still feisty and outspoken, sometimes rude to her siblings and too frequently disdainful of her parents, but she was no longer so self-centered. She'd learned to revere what was good, noble, and heroic and had become more self-disciplined and generous. Her passion for justice and her compassion for people other than herself had been sparked; she was now able to turn her sharp mind and bright spirit toward a worthy goal and to take responsibility for helping others. Rachel's parents hadn't done all that much to help their daughter move from self-absorption to compassionate action, but what they did was critical. They recognized a problem, sought out wise counsel, followed a good suggestion, provided information, and gave their daughter the idea to write a letter to the paper. Those simple steps not only helped their daughter, but also their community. Rachel still needed to learn how to bring her compassion home and treat her family with more respect, but she'd taken a positive step that would likely result in better family relationships over time.

I realize that this story makes it look easy to instill the three Rs. I know that it will not always be so simple. You could rent the same movies that Miriam and Abe rented, and your teenager might refuse to watch them with you. Or you could diligently cut out articles about some local problem and discover that your daughter doesn't care one whit about it. But don't give up! And don't let yourself start nagging or guilt-tripping your son or daughter either. Below are some general tips and suggestions for instilling the three Rs. They won't all work, but your gentle and compassionate persistence will help your adolescent develop humane attitudes and behaviors even if you don't immediately see the effects of your efforts.

Tips for instilling the three Rs in your teenager

Nurturing reverence

- Make a point of bringing the suffering of others, whether humans or animals, into your teenager's sphere of awareness. You can do this by sharing stories at the dinner table, renting videos like Miriam and Abe, or joining a social justice organization and reading its literature.
- Maintain your family's commitment to spending time together outside, and model time alone in natural settings or parks so that your teenager knows she can find solitude and renewal in the natural world. Find opportunities to nurture your own wonder and compassion so that you can be a role model for reverent appreciation.
- Stay aware of local events so that together you and your teenager can discuss what is happening in your neighborhood and community.
- Invite your teenager to inspire you. If your adolescent knows that his concerns and thoughts matter to you, he

will be more likely to share them, and his reverence will be reinforced by your appreciation and involvement.

Instilling respect

- Invite your adolescent to choose some of the ways in which your family will give to others, whether through volunteering, raising money, or donating services.
- Be ever more respectful of your teenagers and model respect for others. Gently point out ways in which they can be more respectful, and help them consider other people's points of view.
- Invite your teenager to teach and lead you toward more respectful lifestyles.

Instilling responsibility

- Let your teenager know that his dollar is his vote. Even though he can't vote in elections until he's 18, you can teach him that he votes every time he spends his money. Teaching our adolescents that they have enormous "voting" power through their spending choices will help them learn to take responsibility for their voting dollars.
- Make explicit the expectations of every family member so that your teenagers understand that each person in the family has certain responsibilities for which they must be accountable.
- Share and celebrate the successes and achievements of your efforts and those of others so that your adolescents will see that people *can* make a difference.
- Express your appreciation for your teenager's efforts to be responsible. Your thanks and recognition will go a long way toward helping your adolescent feel positive about being responsible.

Responsibility is the last of the three Rs, and its attainment is one of the most important goals of adolescence. Your efforts to instill reverence starting in the early years and to inspire respect starting in the middle years will now bear fruit and lead toward more and more responsible behaviors in the teenage years. If you have provided your child with good information, sound critical thinking skills, and a core of reverence and respect, it is very likely that you will have a responsible adolescent. She may not be responsible in every way, but if she understands that her choices matter, she will learn to be responsible in the *important* ways. But once again, modeling the message is key. The more your own life bears the mark of responsible citizenship, the easier it will be for your teenager to understand that she, too, is being called upon to take her reverence and respect and turn it into responsible actions.

ELEMENT 4: PROVIDING POSITIVE CHOICES

LEON, MARTHA AND BEN

Every summer since he was twelve, Ben worked hard to earn money. He knew that he was going to have to pay for most of his college tuition just as his sister Samantha did. At seventeen, however, he was tired of working at the factory where his dad built modular houses. The money was great, more than he could earn as a teenager elsewhere, but it was backbreaking work, and he wanted to do something different. His parents, Leon and Martha, listened to Ben as he talked about taking the summer off and going on a bike trip with his friends. They wanted Ben to have the same opportunities as his more affluent peers, but they also knew that if Ben went on the bike trip, he would not only spend money but also not earn the four thousand dollars he could make in a summer at the factory.

They asked Ben questions about all the things he'd like to do, about how it would feel to have that much less money for college, about his dreams and hopes for the future. They expressed genuine interest in finding out what was important to him and in helping him decide what to do over the summer. They didn't tell him he had to work with his dad, and they let him know that the decision would ultimately be up to him, but they suggested that he might be able to find some exciting and worthwhile opportunities that still enabled him to earn money.

His parents' questions got Ben thinking. He really was worried about having less money for college. The bike trip sounded like fun, but when he thought about what really excited him about the trip, he realized that it was the part about biking in Yellowstone National Park. His family had been to Yellowstone when he was ten, and he'd loved it and thought it would be great to go back. He'd been amazed at the wildlife, the geysers, and the topography. When he talked to his parents later, his eyes lit up when he spoke about Yellowstone, and Martha and Leon recognized that their son had a real passion for Wyoming and the national park.

"Perhaps you could get a job there," Martha said. "I bet they hire lots of people in the summer." Ben contacted the park service and was able to get a job as a busboy at a restaurant. The pay wasn't great, but he'd earn $1,700 (after his travel and living expenses) and still have most of his days free. He also found out about volunteer opportunities to study wildlife during the day.

Ben had a fantastic summer. His busboy job wasn't much fun, but he learned so much volunteering. The leader of the project, Brad Williams, became an important role model for Ben. Ben had never considered how his personal choices were affecting the environment before that summer. Brad taught Ben how to live more simply and how to make personal decisions that caused less harm, and Ben felt really good about taking responsibility for his choices. He changed his diet so that he was eating lower on the food chain and committed to reducing his use of fossil fuels and to repairing and reusing materials rather than buying things he really didn't need. He realized that he could save a lot of money during the coming year, too, by living more simply, getting clothes at thrift shops, and borrowing and sharing things with friends. Ben had always been fairly self-disciplined but somewhat somber. Now that he had a direction that excited and engaged him, he became enthusiastic and happy. His ability to persevere and act with integrity, coupled with his enthusiasm and commitment to environmental concerns, turned him into a leader.

When Ben returned for his senior year in high school, he volunteered to chair the floundering environmental club. He took an environmental science elective, stayed in touch with Brad, who wrote him an excellent recommendation for college, and in May heard that he'd received a scholarship from one of the colleges that he'd applied to.

Like all parents, Martha and Leon wanted what was best for their child, but they knew that they didn't know exactly what "best" looked like. They invited Ben to participate in discovering a good choice for his last summer in high school, recognizing that while he needed to make money, he also needed to pursue interests beyond his lucrative summer job at the factory. They asked Ben questions and helped him figure out a positive choice that had long-term benefits even though it didn't make him as much money. By helping Ben see that he had choices beyond the drudgery of another year at the factory or a summer off to bike and play, they helped Ben realize a greater dream.

Ben's summer at Yellowstone and his relationship with a mentor also provided new choices, and with guidance Ben was able to make healthy and wise decisions that had an impact long after the summer was over. By recognizing Ben's interests and encouraging positive choices, his parents helped him become empowered as a leader. In addition, Ben's choices were helping the environment.

During adolescence, our children will be making many of their own decisions. By the time they leave home we can only hope that we have given them solid information, taught them good critical thinking skills, instilled the three Rs, and modeled enough of the best qualities that the decisions they make will be humane.

Most of us are concerned that our adolescent children make good choices in relation to their safety, their health, and their future, but humane choices demand more than this. While we parents may initially be more worried about our teenagers making wise decisions regarding such issues as sexuality, drugs, alcohol, schoolwork, friends, and future careers, we need to remember that raising a humane child requires that our teenagers have the tools to make fully humane choices in relation to everyone and everything. You can help your adolescent become a wise and compassionate choice-maker by routinely examining choices in your home. Instead of making most of the decisions yourself, you can ask your teenagers which choices they think would be best. You can invite them to consider choices based on family health and welfare as well as on human rights, environmental concerns and animal protection. Here are some issues where participating in the decision-making process can empower your adolescent:

- What foods should the family have in the house?
- What stores should the family shop at?
- What service work should the family do?
- What kind of vacation should the family go on, taking into consideration individual interests and desires, costs, and the vacation's effects on others (people, animals, and the Earth)?
- What summer activities should the teenagers engage in, what jobs should they have?
- What household chores should they take on?

By inviting your teenager's voice and involvement in these decisions, you demonstrate your respect for him and inspire him to meet your expectations.

WHAT TO DO WHEN
YOU FIND HARDCORE PORNOGRAPHY
IN YOUR 16-YEAR-OLD SON'S ROOM

a) Give yourself time to respond
Avoid talking to your son about the pornography until you've had time to carefully consider the best way to respond.

b) Elements 1 and 2: Gather information and think critically
Talk to respected parents or professionals and read about the effects of pornography on teens. While it is normal for teens to find, read, and view pornography, it's important to ask what the consequences of such exposure might be. Pornography can have a negative impact on how your son views sexuality and relationships, and you'll need to think carefully about how to handle this issue to make sure you have the skills to talk to your son without shaming him. By reading, researching, and reflecting you will gain the information and skills you need.

c) Elements 3 and 4: Use the three Rs and make a positive choice
You can use the discovery of pornography as an opportunity to discuss sexuality (just like one of the mothers in the Introduction did), and to teach your son that reverence, respect, and responsibility are essential components of healthy sexual relationships. Whether or not you confront your son with your discovery, you can still discuss sexuality and pornography with him. The discussion can be a general foray into the subject in which you examine the

concept of pornography with a critical eye and consider the effects of pornography on people's perception of sexuality and intimate relationships. Finding pornography may be the impetus you were waiting for to initiate an important conversation with your son. While you (and your son) may feel embarrassed to have such a frank discussion, it may pave the way for your son's reverence for the sacredness of sex, his respect for those with whom he will have intimate relationships, and his sense of responsibility if he is or when he becomes sexually active.

d) Stay flexible and be prepared to revisit the issue
You will not be able to forbid pornography, but you can find "teachable moments" during your son's adolescence in which you raise questions, share pertinent articles, and invite your son to be a more aware consumer of pornography if he continues to view and read it. Your input may well diminish his susceptibility to damaging attitudes and future negative behaviors.

IT'S NEVER TOO LATE TO HELP A TEENAGER BE HUMANE

If the early years were the time to build the foundation and the middle years the time to carefully lay the bricks, adolescence is the time to furnish the house with the nuanced details of humane living before our children are ready to take what they've learned and move into their own homes. But even if we have failed to build the strongest foundation or have laid the bricks haphazardly, it is not too late. Together with our teenager we can patch the problem areas, fix the leaks, and still make the house the most humane home it can be before their time with us is done. Unless we have seriously neglected or abused our children, the door is practically always open to keep trying.

As I am writing this in my home in coastal Maine, another metaphor comes to mind. Raising a humane child is like a ship's journey on a beautiful, mysterious, yet sometimes perilous ocean. The Four Elements can be your rudder. All you really need to do is steer. At times, gale force winds will make it seem nearly impossible to maintain your course. Then there will be times when the seas are calm, and all you need is the barest grip. You may even forget that you need to steer at all until a rogue wave comes and unexpectedly rocks the boat. There will also be times when you thought you charted the perfect course until you realize that the map failed to show the sharp ledges in your path. Each time your equilibrium is challenged, each time the weather changes, you can grasp the rudder, relying upon your steady hand to stay your course.

SEVEN

THE CHILD BECOMES A HUMANE ADULT

May your life preach more loudly than your lips.

— WILLIAM ELLERY CHANNING

For the last chapter of this book, I thought it would be useful (and hopefully inspiring and validating) to hear the stories of some humane young adults and read about the ways in which their parents taught them to embody the best qualities of human beings. I chose to interview those people, now in their late teens or twenties, who began to live according to humane values at a young age, during childhood or adolescence. I asked how their parents helped them become the humane people they are today. What they told me reinforced my belief in the power of parents to raise humane children.

Most of the people I interviewed I know well, but a couple of them I only know from the extraordinary work that has made them famous. I wanted you to "meet" a variety of young people, some well known for humanitarian work, others leading unpublicized but deeply humane lives. It's my hope that their stories will strengthen your conviction that your choices, your parenting, and your modeling matter profoundly. Being humane is not synonymous with being an activist, but deeply humane people cannot help but strive to improve the world for others; and if you raise your children to be humane, it is likely that they will naturally try to help make the world better, like the young men and women you'll meet now.

OCEAN ROBBINS

Ocean Robbins was born in a one-room log cabin in British Columbia. His parents, John and Deo Robbins, had built the cabin themselves. For seven years, they grew much of their food and lived harmoniously on only $6,000 a year. When Ocean was of school age, however, they realized that he would be better served in a community with more children, and they heard about an alternative school in Vancouver that reflected their family's values.

Although John Robbins had grown up as the only son of Irvin Robbins, founder of Baskin-Robbins ice cream, and was heir to the family business, John had walked away from their ice cream cone-shaped swimming pool as a young man. He did not want a trust fund, nor did he want to inherit the family fortune, and so when it was time to send Ocean to school, cost significantly limited their options. Fortunately, the school they found for Ocean was public.

I asked Ocean what he remembered from his childhood that helped him become humane. He shared the following stories:

One day, at the age of six, he was walking on the beach with his dad when they saw a mother yelling at and slapping her child, a boy who appeared to be about four years old. John turned to Ocean and told him that even though what the mother was doing was awful, she must be suffering herself in order to be doing such a hurtful thing to her son. He explained to Ocean that people only hurt others if they themselves have been hurt — a brief lesson in the cycle of violence — and told him that it was important that someone say "enough hurting."

That might have been the end of the story, an effort by a father to explain abuse to his shocked son, but John didn't just say "enough hurting;" he walked up to the mother and said, "Excuse me, it looks like you're having a hard time, and I was wondering if we could be of any help." The angry mother responded, "It's none of your business!" Calmly, John agreed. "I know it's none of our business, but if we can help, we'd be happy to." The mother began to cry and told John and Ocean that she'd just broken up with her son's dad and that her son had been awful. John told her that he didn't really think that anyone was awful. As John spoke to the mother, Ocean walked up to the boy, pulled a toy car out of his pocket, and asked if he wanted to play. The two children played on the beach for a while as John and the mom continued their conversation. Eventually it was time to part, and Ocean handed the boy his toy car to keep and watched the boy's face light up.

Ocean describes this experience as love in action. His father didn't make someone else bad, but nor did he walk by and ignore the suffering in front of him. Ocean learned several powerful lessons that day. The first lesson was that there are no bad people, just people who have been hurt. He also learned that love requires action, "a strong 'no' as well as a strong 'yes.'" He was taught that it was not all right to ignore suffering. Shortly after this incident, Ocean began trying to help right wrongs, too. When he was seven, his father told him about the nuclear threat. Having learned that it was important to do something to combat danger or injustice, Ocean organized a rally at school with a few friends.

When Ocean was eight, his parents modeled another humane quality for their son: generosity. John was acquainted with a mother and son who were having a particularly difficult time. The mom knew she was parenting badly, but she was in desperate need of time to heal. John and Deo offered to take in this woman's son for two months while she did what she needed to do to get back on her feet. They asked for a commitment from her that when she returned after those two months, she would parent her son in a whole new way. She made a promise to keep that commitment, and for the next couple of months, her son lived with the Robbins family. I asked Ocean if he had any reservations about welcoming this boy, whom he barely knew, into his life — after all, Ocean was an only child, was incredibly close to his parents, and had never had to share his home with another child. On the contrary, Ocean was delighted to have a playmate and felt for a time that he had a brother. The Robbins family frequently invited people to stay with them, and so Ocean was able to witness this kind of generosity throughout his life.

When Ocean speaks about his parents, he credits them with this: they perceived their son as a small, but fully capable, intelligent, and wise person. Consequently, Ocean grew up believing in his inherent worth, dignity, and ability. He always knew that he could make a difference in the world, and he always knew that he could talk to his parents and that they would listen to him. In fact, John had made a point of saying to Ocean that if ever Ocean did not feel heard, he should tell him, and John would stop everything and listen.

Ocean's childhood was not without its struggles. He felt isolated from his peers because he was different from them. What interested and concerned him weren't action figures and television shows. He wanted to talk about deeper topics, but his friends thought of themselves as "just kids" who were meant to play. Ocean pretended to be a regular kid at school, but it was really only at home where he felt he could fully be himself.

In 1988, when he was fourteen, Ocean facilitated a youth summit on the environment in Moscow. While it was an amazing experience to meet Mrs. Gorbachev and Soviet young people, what was even more pivotal was meeting the other American teens on the trip who, like Ocean, cared about the world and wanted to improve it, protect it, and restore it. Shortly after Ocean's trip to the Soviet Union, he conceived of YES! (Youth for Environmental Sanity), an organization dedicated to creating a peaceful world for all. With several friends, Ocean created the YES! Tour, a traveling youth production for secondary school assembly programs that presents environmental, social justice, and animal protection issues through a lively, positive, empowering show. YES! has grown into a thriving youth organization, offering summer camps as well as youth leadership training. In ten years YES! has reached over half a million young people, inspiring them to help create a better world.

Ocean is now married and the father of twin boys. He told me that he makes a point of speaking "straight talk" with his babies each day. He apologizes if he's been grouchy or if he hasn't been the best father he could be that day, the father that they deserve. He tells them how he's feeling or what he's thinking. He knows his sons don't speak yet, but on another level, he knows that they understand him. He won't pretend that they are less than they are: harbingers of a better world.

KHALIF WILLIAMS

I met twenty-nine-year-old Khalif Williams when he attended a weekend workshop on humane living that I was leading. Although there were about forty participants, Khalif stood out.

He was so attentive and engaged, and his eyes were riveted on whoever was speaking. When he spoke, it was with a wisdom and maturity unusual for someone his age. He also brought a fervent enthusiasm to the workshop, a passionate desire to learn, and an openness to listen to all points of view.

About a year and a half later, Khalif emailed me because he and his partner, Amy, were considering a move to Maine. Coincidently, we had a job opening at our organization, The International Institute for Humane Education (IIHE), and I encouraged Khalif to apply. We never did interview anyone else for the position because it was clear after our interview with Khalif that we had found a remarkable man to join our team.

Khalif came to IIHE with a background in social work. He had worked with developmentally disabled adults and had been a counselor at a residential treatment facility for adolescent boys with mental illnesses and behavioral disorders. He had also led a minority mentoring program to help at-risk inner-city youth and worked at an emergency runaway and homeless shelter for teenagers. In the couple of years before joining IIHE, he had also started his own farm animal refuge and humane education program, which he ran as a volunteer.

I asked Khalif how his parents helped him to become the deeply humane, incredibly hard-working and committed person he is today, and he shared some stories. He told me about his mother's unconditional love, not only for her family but also for the stray dogs she periodically adopted. Khalif actually grew up disliking dogs because so many of the family dogs were difficult and destructive (however, Khalif is now the guardian of two rescued dogs whom he adores). Khalif's mom loved their dogs unconditionally despite the fact that they peed in the house, destroyed the furniture, and sometimes even bit. She didn't abandon them, but cared for them even though they severely taxed her patience. Khalif credits his mother's ability to love even the most difficult of beings with his growing appreciation for what love means and requires. He learned from her that

relationships are not meant to serve his personal needs and con-
venience but demand patience, care, and compassion. He also
credits his mother's example for his later interest in and success
at working with adolescents with behavioral problems: "These
kids were so aggressive and difficult, but I learned from my
mother how to love them no matter how they behaved."

I asked Khalif about his father, and he told me the following
story: When he was about ten, he and his brother were watching
the news on television and were making fun of some of the people being interviewed by the newscasters. They were calling them
rednecks and making insulting comments about those who were
fat or had teeth missing or seemed to them to be stupid, when his
father, Floyd, came in the room. He asked his sons, "Why are you
talking that way? What do you know about these people? Do you
hate people who are fat or have no teeth?" Khalif responded that
he didn't, and his dad simply replied, "That's how it sounds."
Khalif's father didn't berate his sons; instead he questioned them,
and he explained that harmful attitudes can lead to harmful
behaviors.

Floyd Williams was accustomed to being stereotyped himself.
He was a black man married to a white woman living in a predominantly white city in northwestern Pennsylvania. His mixed-
race sons were also used to being stereotyped and faced the challenges of racism regularly. It was not hard for Khalif to understand the dangers of judging people based on their appearance,
and his father's words struck a deep chord and have stayed with
him ever since.

Floyd was a staunch advocate of being your own person. He
constantly encouraged Khalif to question everything, to take
nothing at face value, to determine for himself what was right or
wrong, and, most of all, to trust his own heart and intuition to
discover who he was. Floyd emphasized that what was important
was who Khalif was: what he did, what he valued, and whether he
was kind. He explained to Khalif that what was on the outside
didn't matter; what was on the inside did.

Floyd offered Khalif plenty of role models and mentors on the path to discovering who he was. He gave him books like the *Tao Te Ching*, and readings by Kahlil Gibran. He encouraged Khalif to seek out people with knowledge and taught him *how* to think rather than *what* to think. He periodically gave Khalif puzzles to solve that would last for months, even years, encouraging Khalif to come up with answers to the riddles himself, rather than rely on his father to solve the problem.

As Khalif shared with me these stories about his dad, I couldn't help but smile. These stories explained Khalif's ardent pursuit of truth. Floyd had led his son on a spiritual quest, and Khalif is still following the path with integrity, honesty, and soul-searching. Floyd had laid a foundation of truth-seeking in his son that had helped Khalif grow into the open, inquisitive, and committed person I had come to know.

Floyd died when Khalif was only twenty, but Khalif still learns from him. When he asks his father for advice, he hears a wise answer. Khalif recalled a strange and lucid dream he had right after his father died. In the dream his father was walking in the cemetery where he was about to be buried when he said to Khalif, "As long as you are true to yourself, you will always have me."

MEETING CARRIE AND DAVID

Carrie Lang and David Berman were both twelve years old when I met them. They had signed up for one of the humane education courses I taught at the University of Pennsylvania summer program for secondary school students. The next summer I was delighted to see Carrie again, in another course I was teaching. After that second summer was over, I got a phone call from David's mother, Ellen. She had encouraged David to take a course with a different teacher that summer and regretted it because David hadn't enjoyed the course as much as he had the summer before. She was calling me to ask if I would consider teaching another course that David could take after school. As we talked, it became apparent that Ellen didn't agree with some of the things I'd taught her son. For one, her training as a physician had left her with a different opinion about the ethics and worth of animal testing, a topic we had discussed one day in class. For another, her son's shift to vegetarianism in a meat-eating household created more work for her. Surprised by her desire to have me continue as her child's teacher, I asked her why she was so enthusiastic about my course and why she wanted me to teach David during the school year. "Are you kidding?" she responded. "He's not into drugs, and he wants to change the world!" Ellen recognized that her son was entering adolescence, separating and making his own decisions. She honored his transition. As long as he wasn't hurting himself or others, she enthusiastically supported the unfolding of her son's true self. I had so much admiration for her, and for the ways in which she lived in harmony with her son even though she didn't share all of his convictions.

I did offer to teach an after-school course at David's mother's suggestion, and because the students interested in the course came from several different schools, we held it in my living room. Carrie and David brought some of their friends, and soon they were inspired to start their own group that they named S.P.A.R.E. (Students Protecting Animals' Rights and the Environment). S.P.A.R.E. educated their peers, arranged talks at their schools, participated in protests and letter-writing campaigns, volunteered at nonprofit organizations, and grew to include hundreds of local students.

Although I have stayed in touch with Carrie throughout the years, I lost touch with David for quite a while. One day I heard from him. He'd graduated from college, where he'd been active in human rights efforts, and was emailing me from Jamaica where he was working as a Peace Corps volunteer. As I write this, David is completing two master's degrees in Public Health and Public Policy Administration, and Carrie has just graduated from nursing school. I talked to Carrie and David to find out more about their childhood experiences and the ways their parents raised them to be so humane.

CARRIE LANG

Most of the vacations in Carrie's family were spent either camping or at Carrie's grandmother's house in rural Connecticut. Carrie's grandmother (her father's mother) loved nature, and her home was filled with Petersen's guides and other books about animals and plants. Visits were punctuated by exclamations when unusual birds alighted on branches near the house, but one visit in particular stands out in Carrie's memory. A family of beavers moved onto her grandmother's land, and the whole vacation was spent marveling at the extraordinary engineering of these animals. Carrie remembers that the dominant emotions in the household were excitement and gratitude. "We all felt so lucky," Carrie told me. Carrie thought that her family's response was typical, but when she told other people about the beavers, most suggested that Carrie's grandmother trap or poison them because beavers were so destructive. It was true that the beavers were chewing down trees, but Carrie's grandmother never begrudged the beavers their food or shelter. The family became more careful about where they planted new trees, but they never once considered harming the beavers or trying to evict them.

Carrie's parents and grandmother instilled in her and her sisters a reverence for nature that was deep and sustaining. They taught her to respect all animals, including insects. In fact, Carrie learned never to crush bugs, but to appreciate them without interfering with their lives. The overriding principle was, "Do no harm." But the reverence cultivated in Carrie went well beyond nature and animals. Carrie's parents, aunts, and Granny (her mother's mother) were all socially conscious and politically active, and Carrie was taught from an early age to question different viewpoints, recognize the perspectives of others around the world, and not assume that everything she read in the newspaper was completely accurate. Holiday gatherings included lively discussions about nonviolent political activism and efforts on behalf of civil rights. Both of Carrie's parents had been Peace

Corps volunteers, and both encouraged Carrie to take pride in any work she did to better the world and help others.

Dinner was a time for debate and discussion, and everyone's opinions were welcome at the table. As Carrie and her sisters grew up, their parents were open to what they might learn from their daughters, and Carrie always felt that her views, even when they diverged from her parents, were encouraged. When, at the age of twelve, Carrie told her parents that she wanted to be a vegetarian, they not only supported her decision, they modified the family's meals accordingly. They were willing to change their household traditions when their young daughter made an ethical decision. Neither of Carrie's parents became vegetarian themselves, but they honored Carrie's choice and helped her live according to her values.

Good citizenship was an important value in the Lang household, and Carrie accompanied her parents to the voting booth at each and every election. Her parents taught her that voting was both a privilege and a responsibility, and when Carrie turned eighteen, she registered immediately — and has never missed an election, major or minor. Carrie was always encouraged to do volunteer work as a child, too, and to distribute food to those less fortunate.

When Carrie was in third grade, she recalls making a derogatory joke about a girl she knew who had a physical disability. Her parents were very angry with her and let her know that such comments were completely unacceptable and wrong. Carrie remembers feeling quite ashamed, but the event stands out clearly as pivotal. She assumed that that was how all children were raised and was shocked to realize that in some other families insulting other people was acceptable. Many years later, at a friend's house, Carrie was stunned when the whole family began making jokes about another person who was overweight. She was the only person in the room who wasn't laughing.

Carrie never lacked for toys, but her parent's attitude about material possessions was obvious in the small birthday parties they planned for her and the implicit focus on relationships between people rather than on the acquisition of things. They taught their children to think about others rather than to focus solely on themselves. Carrie's parents bought much of their children's clothes at the Salvation Army, never at fancy department stores. For a brief period in middle school, Carrie was embarrassed about her second-hand clothes, but the ethic of thrift stayed with her, and by high school, finding great clothes at thrift shops had become a value of her own.

Carrie's family was involved in their local Unitarian Universalist Church, and Carrie grew up in the embrace of a religion that taught tolerance and encouraged social action. She stayed involved in the church youth group throughout high school, participating in efforts to promote social justice throughout her teenage years. At the beginning of high school, Carrie's dad invited her to come with him to a march in Washington, DC. A city planner and college professor, Carrie's father had been writing a book on homelessness, and traveling to Washington to participate in a march for affordable housing was a part of what it meant to live according to one's ethics and to work for a more just world.

Ever since I have known Carrie I have been impressed by her quiet, thoughtful intelligence and her deep compassion. She has always seemed older than her years, more wise than others her age, but well-liked and popular with whatever group she was with. What struck me as I got to know Carrie was that she pondered everything deeply, brought a critical eye to all issues, debated them, and always consulted with her deepest values before coming to an opinion about an issue or action. I have never heard her speak ill of anyone. I admire Carrie tremendously, and as I listened to her share stories about her childhood and her upbringing, many of the pieces of her extraordinary spirit made perfect sense. It was clear from talking with her about her parents that they had helped her in very important ways to become the humane person she is today. When Carrie talked to her mother about our interview, her mother was adamant that she didn't want to take credit for who Carrie has become, and she told Carrie that she always believed that her children were born with good hearts. But aren't all children born with good hearts? Carrie's parents fostered the development and direction of their children's hearts, and all their daughters are living examples of what can happen when parents raise humane children.

Today Carrie is married to a kind, bright, and gentle man. She is training to be a midwife. She plans to have children of her own, and to raise them with the values she was taught by her parents.

DAVID BERMAN

When I spoke with David, now twenty-seven, about the ways in which his parents nurtured humane values, his gratitude toward and appreciation of them was very moving. He remembered growing up feeling incredibly supported by his parents who encouraged his independence and gave him freedom to pursue his interests, even when they conflicted with their own. For example, when he was in high school David wanted to attend a protest against an animal experimenter's research at the medical school where his mom was a professor. The issue of animal experimentation was very polarized at the University, and allegiances were important, yet David's parents did not discourage David from attending the protest; in fact, they drove him there.

David's parents taught him to think for himself, to remain open, and to respect other people's points of view. He recalls that they never passed judgment but were sensitive and good listeners who encouraged him to be active in the world. They were always rooting for him, but they didn't coddle or cater to their son. When he announced that he was going to be a vegetarian, they told him that he would be responsible for making his own meals. David now credits them with his ability to cook. He has fond memories of cooking side by side with his mother. David's parents responded differently to their son's vegetarianism than Carrie's, but both approaches worked well. While Carrie's parents changed their meal preparation to honor their daughter's ethics, David's mother insisted that David cook his own meals, fostering his sense of responsibility and the quality of self-discipline.

David's parents were politically and socially active people. Family dinners were lively and engaging. They also created a community around David. Although not particularly religious, they sent David to a Hebrew school, which provided him with a model of compassion that emphasized social action.

David's sense of freedom and self-confidence may have stemmed in large part from the constant support of his parents. They did not urge David to follow the dreams they had for him, but rather to pursue his own goals. They applauded his concern with animal protection, environmental issues, and world affairs, and they always let him know how proud and appreciative they were of him.

Since college David has been actively involved in social justice issues, particularly AIDS work. As he completes his graduate studies, I have no doubt that David will make a profound contribution to the world. His commitment to help others runs deep. He is grounded and passionate, and knows who he is and what really matters.

DANNY SEO

Danny Seo, an activist and author of several books, was described by *People Magazine* in 1999 as "the world's most amazing 22-year-old." The youngest child of Korean immigrants, Danny grew up in Reading, Pennsylvania. He initially described his parents as stoic people who were extremely concerned with their children's academic success. Danny watched his older brother and sister graduate from high school with 4.0 grade point averages and head off to Ivy League colleges, and he knew that he was meant to follow the same path. Instead, Danny found himself drawn in a different direction. He became extremely concerned about environmental problems and animal suffering, and when he was twelve years old started a youth group called Earth 2000 to combat injustice and ecological degradation. His parents were not particularly interested in these causes and, in fact, secretly hoped that Danny was simply going through a phase. Then Danny's grades began to drop. No longer a straight A student, he began getting Ds and even an occasional F, but he wasn't depressed or unmotivated. On the contrary, he asked his mother to drop him off at the library every afternoon where he poured over *Advertising Age* magazine, books on marketing, public relations treatises, and whatever else he could get his hands on to learn how to get his ideas and his values into mainstream culture.

Danny took what he learned and put it into practice, turning Earth 2000 into one of the most successful youth organizations in the world. The organization, and the issues it championed, were gaining significant media attention, and teenage Danny Seo was becoming famous.

Danny's parents knew that their son was fine, even though his values differed from their own. While *they* wanted him to be academically successful, Danny wanted to be successful at changing the world. They recognized that their son was living his life with profound integrity and courage even though his interests and dreams were so different from their own. They could have stopped him, but they didn't. They let their teenage boy succeed or fail on his own, taking a back seat rather than becoming "stage parents" for their activist son.

Danny learned from his parents that he was accountable for everything he did. If a campaign succeeded, it was because he and his friends made the success happen. If it failed, he had to learn what he did wrong and try again. Danny has become, by all accounts, tremendously successful. He chose not to go to college because he had too much work to do, and by age twenty-four he had published four books, created several successful companies that sell environmentally friendly products, become a bestselling author and national icon in Korea, and made fundraising for non-profits part and parcel of his life.

How did his parents contribute to Danny's incredible success? Despite their conservative values, Danny's parents were actually both somewhat rebellious themselves. His mother's family had been hostile toward institutionalized religion, yet Danny's mother found a way to sneak off to Church and cultivate a deeply spiritual life. His father's emigration from Korea was shocking to his grandparents, yet he followed his dream and made it real. His parents made choices in order to live according to their deepest values, and in so doing they modeled perseverance, commitment, and integrity. However much Danny's specific choices came to differ from theirs, it was this modeling that mattered, and Danny now embodies the qualities of integrity and dedication so deeply that his life is a full expression of these virtues.

Every Christmas Danny's family participated in a church program to give gifts to people less fortunate. From age five, Danny remembers his parents taking him to the store where he would use his own money to buy gifts for people he would never see. He would wrap the gifts himself and bring them to Church. What he remembers most from this annual tradition was how good it made him feel to be generous and giving. That generosity has become a hallmark of Danny's life.

When I asked Danny what it was like to grow up different from his peers, he admitted that he enjoyed being different. He felt in many ways that he was able to discover who he was at a very young age. While his friends wondered what they would do with their lives in the future, Danny was busy doing what was right and true to him in the present. Peer pressure was a non-issue for him because he knew who he was. In fact, in eighth grade his geography teacher told him that even though a lot of students and teachers thought Danny was kind of crazy, he was proud of him for having such a tough skin. Danny didn't know what his teacher was talking about. He was oblivious to anyone's opinion of his lifestyle choices or activism. He had half a dozen close friends and purpose in life, and negative opinions didn't register.

One day in high school, Danny, the only Asian-American in his school, opened his locker to discover that the contents had been stolen and the locker marked with racial slurs. His first thought was, "I don't need this today." He was in the midst of one of his various campaigns, and the timing for this vandalism was terrible. He went to the principal and accepted the principal's suggestion to use a shelf instead of a locker from then on. It wasn't ideal, but he had other battles to fight and much more important places to put his energy.

One might imagine that Danny exists in his own world, and lives and breathes his work. One might suspect that his stubborn determination manifests itself in a fiery, passionate, perhaps even controlling personality. Quite the contrary. I have known Danny since he was a teenager, and I have always found him to be warm, somewhat soft-spoken, often quiet, yet always busy figuring out how he can help the people he's talking to and advance the cause of peace and justice. He does this in an easy-going and unassuming way. There is a calm quality to him as he goes about busily scheming ways to improve life for everyone.

DANI DENNENBERG

Dani Dennenberg is twenty-six years old, a student in our affiliated M.Ed. program in humane education, a recipient of a grant to offer humane education programs in San Diego county, and a good friend. Dani embodies a rare combination of passionate commitment to end suffering and planetary destruction and a deep and abiding respect for others' beliefs and opinions. I have never seen Dani behave in a self-righteous, dogmatic, or proselytizing manner. Instead, she is warm, inviting, and respectful of the opinions of others. These qualities make her a wonderful teacher.

When I asked Dani to tell me about the ways in which her parents helped her become the person she is today, she quickly focused on the Golden Rule. Her mother stressed that Dani should "do unto others what she would have them do unto her" and that "she should not do unto others what she would not want done to her." This Golden Rule, coupled with her father's strong work ethic, determination, and perseverance, produced a beautiful alchemy in Dani. She is deeply committed to improving the world, possessing an intense will, yet she carries with her a kindness and compassion toward everyone, even those who disagree with her or who actively cause harm and suffering.

Growing up with the qualities of commitment and caring led Dani to become a vegetarian when she was in tenth grade. Her identical twin, Hava, followed suit within a couple of months. Their parents were very supportive of their teenage girls and simply wanted to ensure that the girls did the research necessary to eat a healthy diet. During their senior year in high school they were faced with having to dissect an animal heart. Dani knew immediately that she could not, in good conscience, participate in something that ran counter to her beliefs, and with her parents' support she approached her teacher with both trepidation and resolve. As she expected, her teacher was angry, and although she let Dani and Hava opt out of the sheep heart dissection, she required that they each write a lengthy research paper on myocardial infarction (heart attacks). Although Dani felt that the assignment was unfair, requiring far more work than her dissecting classmates had to do, she also knew that she would learn a lot from it. This passion for learning is integral to Dani's character and a large part of what makes her both a great student and a great teacher.

What Dani was unprepared for was the response of some students. Although she and Hava had sometimes been teased for their vegetarian diet, she always felt that it was fine to be different. Her parents had taught her to stand up for her beliefs and stick to her commitments, and she knew that most of her peers actually admired her for living according to her convictions. When a boy from her class put a sheep's heart on her car she was unprepared for such hostility. She burst into tears, but she and

Hava told no one. Word got around, however, and the boy who did it apologized to Dani. That same night, their teacher called. She'd heard the rumors and asked Dani if she knew who had put the sheep's heart on her car. Dani chose not to tell her teacher. She'd received an apology and had no desire to get her classmate into trouble. Dani had absorbed the value of forgiveness.

Dani's parents were involved in the civil rights movement, and they sent their twin daughters to an integrated magnet school so that their white, Jewish girls would be exposed to a variety of people and cultures. Openness to and respect for others remain integral to Dani's values to this day. Her parents also spoke to Dani about the word *hate* and discouraged her from ever using the word. Dani grew up believing that *hate* was a profanity, and she rarely used it. As she learned about the suffering of animals in factory farms, the destruction of the planet through arrogance, greed, and short-sightedness, and the oppression of people around the world, Dani has always felt deep sorrow, but she doesn't dwell in hate. She dwells in action. And when she is tired or hungry or feels like complaining, she always remembers that there are others who are suffering terribly at the same moment. Whether the other is a starving child, a woman toiling in a sweatshop, or a veal calf in a crate, Dani quickly turns her own frustrations or complaints back into action on behalf of others. This is what her parents taught her.

Dani has turned her compassion and respect for others into a career in humane education. She shares her beliefs with students as she invites them to explore their own. She doesn't tell young people who they should be, what they should believe, or what they should do, but rather she welcomes their search for their own truths and inspires them to make sure that their lives are a full expression of kindness, empathy, and integrity.

Perhaps one of the ways in which Dani is most effective as a teacher is as a listener. Although teachers spend much of their time speaking, the best ones are also superb listeners. Dani learned this skill from her parents, too. She describes her parents as "extraordinary listeners" and says that she rarely felt misunderstood or not heard when she was growing up. She also felt trusted by her parents. Not surprisingly, Dani grew up not only to be extremely trustworthy and reliable but also to be trusting of others and to believe in the good that resides in everyone.

CRAIG KIELBURGER

When Craig Kielburger was twelve years old, he read an article in *The Toronto Star* about the murder of Iqbal Masih, a Pakistani boy, also twelve, who had become an impassioned and powerful spokesperson for children's rights. Iqbal had been sold into slavery at the age of four and for the next six years worked twelve hours a day, six days a week tying knots in rugs. When he finally escaped with the help of a human rights group, he became an eloquent critic of child labor and slavery. The morning Craig read about Iqbal's murder, it was as if Iqbal passed the torch to Craig from his grave. Craig immediately researched the plight of children around the world and began to speak out himself. He formed an organization — Kids can Free the Children — started to raise money to help children in developing countries, and, by the time he entered his teenage years, had became one of the most successful human rights activists of our time.

Craig, now nineteen, has won awards by the armful. According to an article by Shelley Page in *The Ottawa Citizen*, he's the recipient of the Roosevelt Freedom Medal, the State of the World Forum Award, the Governor General's Award for Meritorious Service, the Founders Award, and the Ozaki Memorial Award for promoting justice, alleviating poverty, and contributing to better governance.

This is what Craig has to say about what inspires him to do his work:

> *In many developing countries, children are often asked to work long hours at hazardous jobs with no opportunity to play or to go to school. They are not allowed to*

develop physically, intellectually, and emotionally. They support entire families. They fight in wars. They are given too much responsibility at too young an age. On the other hand, in many industrialized countries, everything is done for children. They are segregated most of their lives with members of their own age group and given little opportunity to assume responsibility, to develop a social conscience. How many games of Super Nintendo do you want to play? How many times do you want to go to the shopping mall? Young people are longing for something more meaningful in their lives, something more challenging, something that allows them to prove themselves.[1]

Craig, himself, provides that something. He has been inspiring young people to help other young people and has created a phenomenally successful organization to help children around the world.

Craig's parents, Fred and Theresa Kielburger, are teachers. They taught Craig and his older brother, Marc, to stand up for what they believe in. They didn't push their sons in any particular direction, but rather they let them choose their own path. Marc, an environmental activist, "broke his parents in," paving the way for Craig to become an activist, too, yet when Craig chose the path of human rights activism, there were times when Fred and Theresa were faced with the unexpected consequences of their own child-rearing philosophy. Even before Craig turned thirteen, Kids can Free the Children had become quite successful, and at the Kielburger household (also the office for Kids can Free the Children), the phones were ringing off the hook. The house was in turmoil. Theresa thought Craig had done enough. He was about to enter eighth grade, and she told Craig that it was time to focus on his studies. She went on to say that while Kids can Free the Children had accomplished so much, Craig needed to get back to normal life. Craig went to his room to think, and didn't come out for a long time. When he did, he told his mother that he couldn't give up now. "You and dad always tell us that we have to fight for what we believe in. Well, I believe in this." He told his mom that he simply couldn't go back to who he was before. He couldn't quit. Theresa understood and gave Craig her full support for his work from then on.

Craig needed to learn and understand more if he was going to make a difference in the lives of abused and exploited children, and he wanted desperately to visit some of the countries where children were sold into slavery to see for himself the plight of young people and to meet those for whom he was speaking. He wanted to witness first-hand the conditions under which children like Iqbal toiled. Craig asked his parents if he could travel to South Asia with his friend Alam Rahman, a University of Toronto student from Bangladesh. Initially Fred and Theresa said no (Craig was only twelve, after all), but in time they agreed under two conditions: Craig had to raise half of the money himself, and he had to convince them that he would be safe. They set the bar high, and Craig met their conditions. While some people thought Craig's parents were crazy to let their twelve-year-old son travel to South Asia with a college student, they had been convinced by their passionate and responsible boy that he would, indeed, be safe. Once he raised the necessary funds, they said he could go.

While Dani was raised with the ethic of the Golden Rule ("Do unto others what you would have them do unto you"), Craig was raised according to the adage, "From those to whom much is given, much is expected in return." Craig grew up feeling enormously fortunate. His parents had come from humble backgrounds, and Craig had heard his maternal grandmother share a story that affected him deeply. She had taught herself how to type when her young husband died, and she went to the local company (Chrysler) to get a job. With no high school diploma, she was not a strong candidate, but she told the interviewer to try her on any skill. Her positive attitude, self-discipline, and persistence paid off, and she was hired. This story, repeated numerous times throughout Craig's childhood, taught him that even when one is down and out one must appreciate one's good fortune and keep trying.

Craig's parents did not have specific rules about curfews or chores. In fact, Craig couldn't remember a single rule that was enforced in the family. Yet there were expectations of Craig and his brother, Marc. They had responsibilities, and they had freedom. They were expected to use the opportunities in their path, and, like Danny Seo, their success (or failure) was up to them. Fred and Theresa neither stood in the way nor directed their children. They supported them when campaigns or efforts failed, and they supported them when they succeeded. They believed in their sons, nurturing them as children, but showing them the respect they accorded adults.

Like so many of the other young adults I interviewed for this chapter, Craig referred to the dinner table. In the Kielburger household it was during supper that issues, concerns, and ideas were raised for discussion. Fred and Theresa shared the news of the day and talked about what was going on in the world. They welcomed their sons' opinions, and through these discussions Craig began to realize his place in the world, and his commitment to use his gifts in the service of others took root.

Some have called Craig an idealist, but he is both a visionary and a man of action. His efforts have been eminently practical. As he says in the *Ottawa Citizen* interview,

> *As young people, we are often called dreamers for hoping that one day there will be a world without war, a world without suffering. The truth is, it was the dreamers who thought that one day we would end the slave trade. It was dreamers who fought so the Berlin Wall would fall. It was dreamers who struggled to end apartheid in South Africa. Just imagine if all the young people ... became involved in a single action to promote peace? Just imagine the power we would have?*

Or imagine if young people, coast to coast, all became involved under one banner for a single action, united in cause promoting peace — we would be unstoppable.[2]

After completing the interviews for this chapter I was struck by the multitude of subtle ways in which parents influence and shape their children's beliefs and values. A reaction to Carrie's derogatory comments in third grade; respectful questioning directed at Khalif when he was ten; an encounter with a child being mistreated when Ocean was six — these incidents remind us that we parents have opportunities to teach our children all the time, and although we do not know exactly when our words, our modeling, or our choices will have the greatest impact, the fact is that what we say and do matters. Our children may not remember many details of how they were parented, but they will be able to recall the salient features, and perhaps they, too, may recollect a single moment when they learned a lesson from us that steered them toward compassion and kindness. But while there will be pivotal moments when we teach our children something that changes the course of their lives, it is the daily rituals that will likely have the biggest influence. Given the repeated emphasis on the dinner time rituals in the lives of these young adults, I'm beginning to think that what happens around the dinner table has more impact than perhaps any other ritual in the lives of our children. It seems that when families share their ideas and values around the table and listen respectfully to each other, the seeds for much humane living are planted. I would not have imagined when I began this book that such a simple routine — dinner time — could be so important. Yet this daily connection with our children, the ritual of caring, stimulating, and open discussion, repeated night after night, matters enormously.

What these interviews also made me realize is how blessed the parents of these young adults are by their children's love and appreciation. But this blessing isn't just good fortune; the parents described in this chapter earned their children's gratitude and respect by how they chose to parent them.

Parents who set out to raise humane children will also become the recipients of their adult children's wisdom and kindness. Their children may one day remind them about the values they once tried so diligently to instill. In *Everyday Blessings: The Inner Work of Mindful Parenting*, authors Myla and Jon Kabat-Zinn share the story of a woman who raised her son to embody the value of respect for people regardless of their heritage or life circumstance. When her son was twenty-three, she went to his apartment building to pick him up and take him out to dinner. Sitting on the sidewalk in front of her son's building was a homeless woman begging. She ignored the woman and averted her eyes, not wanting the woman's suffering to interfere with her happy mood at the prospect of an evening with her son.

A few minutes later, she and her son left the building, and her son walked right over to the homeless woman, handed her some change, and introduced her to his mother. As she describes it, her son was re-teaching her a value she had lost track of, a value she had taught him so many years before.

CONCLUSION

In the introduction to this book I asked you to imagine the newspaper headlines on May 1, 2040. Those imaginary headlines represent a positive vision for the future, but that vision is by no means sure to come true. The headlines of the future could instead be quite grim. Rather than reports about teens raising money for charity, our adult children could be reading about more school shootings. Instead of articles about environmental restoration, there could be articles about environmental catastrophes. In place of news about political and economic stability, there might be news about even more violence in the world.

However, we do have a say about which world our children will inherit, and we also have the power to influence which world they will ultimately create. When we choose to raise our children to be humane, we cultivate in them the qualities that will contribute to the creation of a world in which restoration, generosity, and prosperity take hold and entrenched problems yield to successful and peaceful solutions. In so doing, we help bring about a society in which our children can succeed, thrive, and contribute.

So all our soul-searching and our efforts to raise humane children and bring about such a world are worth it. All our struggles against our inhumane impulses, all our vigilant attention and commitment to be our best, are worth it. It's all worth it because our children and our planet are worth it.

ENDNOTES

CHAPTER 1

1. Quoted in *The Sun*, March 2001, p. 48.
2. Quoted in *The Sun*, August 2001, p. 48.
3. Quoted in *The Sun*, September 2000, p. 48.
4. Quoted in *The Sun*, May 1999, p. 48.
5. J.R.R. Tolkien, *The Fellowship of the Ring*, Ballantine 1965, p. 82.

CHAPTER 2

1. Quoted in *Heron Dance*, November 2002, p. 7.

CHAPTER 3

1. Quoted in *Heron Dance*, November 2002, p. 7.

CHAPTER 7

1. Shelley Page, "Kielburger Revisited," *The Ottawa Citizen*, 6 October 2002.
2. Shelley Page, "Kielburger Revisited," *The Ottawa Citizen*, 6 October 2002.

"MY LIFE IS MY MESSAGE" QUESTIONNAIRE

his questionnaire asks you to think about the qualities that are most important to you and to consider the ways in which you live accordingly, as well as the ways in which you'd like to better embody your values. It invites you to assess these qualities in relation to your loved ones and others outside your circle of family and friends, so that you can chart a course for achieving your vision both at home and in the expansive way that this book envisions. This questionnaire offers you a chance to really explore your dreams for living a kinder life, to consider what holds you back, and to make some commitments to yourself. As you complete it, try to tap into your deepest wisdom and your most ardent hopes for yourself, your children and the world we all share.

As you complete this questionnaire, you'll notice that most questions are divided into three parts:

1) What you currently do
2) What you want to learn/do
3) What steps you will take.

The purpose of this three-part approach is to help you

i) identify the ways in which you already live according to your values,
ii) explore what you need to learn to live better, and
iii) make tangible plans for achieving your goals.

Initially there may not appear to be much difference between ii) and iii). You'll be asked under ii) what you think you need to learn, or what you'd like to change. Then you'll be asked under iii) to write down the steps you will take to follow through. It may seem that you've already done this by articulating your goal. But the purpose of iii) is to make very concrete and very manageable plans for yourself. Questionnaires like this can quickly turn into giant New Year's resolutions that you commit to wholeheartedly on December 31st only to abandon them by the end of January. Please make sure to write down plans for yourself that are easy to carry through and that truly inspire you. You will notice that under iii) I have not given you much room to write. This is to help you make promises to yourself that are small enough so that you can keep them. You may want to photocopy this questionnaire for easier use.

"MY LIFE IS MY MESSAGE" QUESTIONNAIRE

1. The qualities that are most important to me are the following:

_____ _____ _____ _____

_____ _____ _____ _____

_____ _____ _____ _____

2a. My life already reflects the following qualities fairly well:

_____ _____ _____ _____

_____ _____ _____ _____

2b. I would like to live my life so that it reflects the following qualities more deeply:

_____ _____ _____ _____

_____ _____ _____ _____

2c. In order to achieve this goal, I will take the following steps:

_____

_____

con't ...

3a. As a parent I model the following qualities with and for my child:

_____ _____ _____ _____

_____ _____ _____ _____

3b. I would like to model the following qualities more consciously with and for my child:

_____ _____ _____ _____

_____ _____ _____ _____

3c. In order to achieve this goal, I will take the following steps:

_____

_____

4a. (If applicable) I generally embody the following qualities with my spouse:

_____ _____ _____ _____

_____ _____ _____ _____

4b. (If applicable) I would like to cultivate and embody the following qualities more consciously with my spouse in order not only to improve my marriage but also to better model a healthy, loving relationship for my children:

_____ _____ _____ _____

_____ _____ _____ _____

4c. In order to achieve this goal, I will take the following steps:

_____

_____

5a. In relation to my health (physical, emotional, intellectual, spiritual), I take care of myself in the following ways:

_____

_____

_____

_____

5b. I would like to learn/do the following in order to improve my health:

_____

_____

_____

_____

5c. I will take the following steps to improve my health:

_____

_____

6a. In relation to my children's health (physical, emotional, intellectual, spiritual), I help them in the following ways:

_____

_____

_____

_____

6b. I would like to learn/do the following in order to improve my children's health:

_____

_____

_____

_____

6c. I will take the following steps to improve my children's health:

_____

_____

7a. In my interactions outside of the home, my attitudes, behaviors, and relationships reflect the following qualities and virtues:

_____ _____ _____ _____

_____ _____ _____ _____

7b. I would like to learn/do the following in order to improve my attitude, behaviors, and relationships:

_____

_____

_____

_____

7c. I will take the following steps to improve my attitudes, behaviors, and relationships:

_____

_____

8a. In relation to activism and volunteerism, I already do the following:

_____

_____

_____

8b. In relation to activism and volunteerism, I would like to help more in the following ways:

_____

_____

8c. I will take the following steps in order to help others through activism and volunteerism:

_____

_____

9a. In relation to charitable giving and sharing my resources, I contribute in the following ways:

_____

_____

_____

_____

9b. I would like to contribute more in the following ways:

_____

_____

_____

_____

9c. I will take the following steps to contribute more:

_____

_____

10a. In relation to other people (those who farm, work in factories, produce goods and products I use, etc.), I currently make the following choices to prevent others from suffering or being exploited:

_____

_____

_____

_____

10b. In relation to other people (those who farm, work in factories, produce goods and products I use, etc.), I sense/know that I need to learn about the following in order to make choices that better reflect reverence, respect, and responsibility:

_____

_____

_____

_____

10c. I will take the following steps to learn, think critically, and make more humane choices in relation to other people:

_____

_____

11a. In relation to other species (wildlife, those who are in shelters, those who are used for food and clothing, in product testing, in forms of entertainment, etc.), I currently make the following choices to minimize animal suffering and exploitation:

_____

_____

_____

_____

11b. In relation to other species (wildlife, those who are in shelters, those who are used for food and clothing, in product testing, in forms of entertainment, etc.), I sense/know that I need to learn about the following in order to make choices that better reflect reverence, respect, and responsibility:

_____

_____

_____

_____

11c. I will take the following steps to learn, think critically, and make more humane choices in relation to other species:

_____

_____

12a. In relation to the environment (air, salt water, fresh water, land, soil, forests, rainforests, natural resources, etc.), I currently make the following choices to live an environmentally conscious life:

_____

_____

_____

_____

12b. In relation to the environment (air, salt water, fresh water, land, soil, forests, rainforests, natural resources, etc.), I sense/know that I need to learn about the following in order to make choices that better reflect reverence, respect, and responsibility:

_____

_____

_____

_____

12c. I will take the following steps to learn, think critically, and make more humane choices in relation to the environment:

_____

_____

13a. The following are specific areas about which you might sense/know that you need to learn more. If applicable, after each area, write down what you feel you need to learn in order to make more humane decisions.

Television watching: _____

_____

Non-educational video/computer games: _____

_____

Food choices: _____

_____

Household cleaning products: _____

_____

Personal care products: _____

_____

Clothing choices: _____

_____

Large purchase items (cars, appliances, remodeling, home building, etc.): _____

_____

Family recreation: _____

_____

13b. Revisiting this list, write down what steps you plan to take to learn more so that you can make more informed and humane decisions.

Television watching:_____

_____

Non-educational video/computer games: _____

_____

Food choices: _____

_____

Household cleaning products: _____

_____

Personal care products:_____

_____

Clothing choices: _____

_____

Large purchase items (cars, appliances, remodeling, home building, etc.): _____

_____

Family recreation: _____

_____

14. In order to turn the intentions I identified in this questionnaire into practical changes, I will use the following methods to support and discipline myself (this support can be internal — such as starting a meditation practice — or external — such as taking a class or creating a support group — or a combination of both):

_____

_____

_____

_____

15. In order to help my children join me enthusiastically in these efforts, I will do the following to support and inspire them:

_____

_____

_____

_____

16. Imagine a world 40 years from now in which many of the problems we face today have been solved. Your grandchild visits you and asks, "What role did you play to help make the world better?" What would you like to be able to say to your grandchild?

_____

_____

_____

_____

_____

_____

☀

By completing this questionnaire and making some commitments to learn and do more to make your life a better reflection of the three Rs and the qualities most important to you, you've taken a very positive step toward making your life the message you want it to be. The trick will be to maintain your resolve and keep your commitments. If you have a spouse or partner, it will be very helpful if he or she completes this questionnaire, too, so that you can make decisions that support each other's goals.

HELPFUL HINTS: FACTS, STATS, AND LISTS

HEALTH AND DIET: FACTS AND STATISTICS

These statistics are compiled from John Robbins' *The Food Revolution*. While I have not included citations, each statistic is carefully sourced and documented in Robbins' book.

HEALTH AND DIET

- Percentage of adult daily value for saturated fat in one Double Whopper with cheese: 130
- Percentage of eight-year-old child's daily value for saturated fat in one Double Whopper with cheese: more than 200
- Risk of death from heart disease for vegetarians compared to nonvegetarians: half
- Blood cholesterol levels of complete vegetarians (who consume no meat, fish, dairy, or eggs) compared to those of nonvegetarians: 35 % lower
- Ideal blood pressure: 110/79 or less (without medication)
- Average blood pressure of vegetarians: 112/69

- Average blood pressure of nonvegetarians: 121/77
- Incidence of very high blood pressure (over 140/over 90) in meat eaters compared to that in vegetarians: 13 times greater
- Percentage of patients with high blood pressure who are able to completely discontinue use of medications after adopting a low-sodium, low-fat, high-fiber vegetarian diet: 58
- Amount spent annually by Kellogg's to promote Frosted Flakes: $40 million
- Amount spent annually by the dairy industry on the "milk mustache" ads: $190 million
- Amount spent annually by McDonald's to advertise its products: $800 million
- Amount spent annually by the National Cancer Institute to promote the consumption of fruits and vegetables: $1 million
- Annual medical costs in the U.S. directly attributable to meat consumption: $60-120 billion
- Countries with the highest consumption of dairy products: Finland, Sweden, U.S., England
- Countries with the highest rates of osteoporosis: Finland, Sweden, U.S., England
- Daily calcium intake for African-Americans: more than 1,000 mg
- Daily calcium intake for black South Africans: 196 mg
- Hip fracture rate for African-Americans compared to that of black South Africans: 9 times greater
- Calcium intake in rural China: 1/2 that of people in the U.S.
- Bone fracture rate in rural China: 1/5 that of people in the U.S.
- Foods that when eaten produce calcium loss through urinary excretion: animal protein, salt, and coffee
- Amount of calcium lost in the urine of a woman after she has eaten a hamburger: 28 mg

- Amount of calcium lost in the urine of a woman after she has had a cup of coffee: 2 mg
- Number of antibiotics allowed in U.S. cow's milk: 80
- Average American's estimate when asked what percentage of adults worldwide do not drink milk: 1
- Actual percentage of adults worldwide who do not drink milk: 65
- Leading cause of food-borne illness in the U.S.: Campylobacter
- Number of people in the U.S. who become ill with Campylobacter poisoning every day: more than 5,000
- Number of annual Campylobacter-related fatalities in the U.S.: more than 750
- Primary source of Campylobacter bacteria: contaminated chicken flesh
- Percentage of American chickens sufficiently contaminated with Campylobacter to cause illness: 70
- Percentage of American turkeys sufficiently contaminated with Campylobacter to cause illness: 90
- Number of hens in three commercial flocks screened for Campylobacter by University of Wisconsin researchers: 2,300
- Number of hens *not* infected with Campylobacter: 8
- Number of Americans sickened from eating Salmonella-tainted eggs every year: more than 650,000
- Number of Americans killed from eating Salmonella-tainted eggs every year: 600
- Percentage increase in Salmonella poisoning from raw or undercooked eggs between 1976 and 1986: 600
- Amount of antibiotics administered to people in the U.S. annually to treat diseases: 3 million pounds
- Amount of antibiotics administered to livestock in the U.S. annually for purposes other than treating disease: 24.6 million pounds

- Amount of minerals in organic food compared to conventional food:

Calcium	63 % greater
Chromium	78 % greater
Iodine	73 % greater
Iron	59 % greater
Magnesium	138 % greater
Potassium	125 % greater
Selenium	390 % greater
Zinc	60 % greater

- American per capita consumption of soft drinks in 1989: 47 gallons
- American per capita consumption of tap water in 1989: 37 gallons

ANIMAL SUFFERING

- Mass of breast tissue of eight-week-old chicken today compared with 25 years ago: 7 times greater
- Percentage of broiler chickens who are so obese by the age of six weeks that they can no longer walk: 90
- Number of U.S. pigs raised for meat: 90 million
- Number of U.S. pigs raised in total confinement factories where they never see the light of day until being trucked to slaughter: 65 million
- Percentage of U.S. pigs who have pneumonia at time of slaughter: 70

ENVIRONMENTAL CONCERNS

- Amount of water required to produce 1 pound of California foods, according to Soil and Water specialists, University of California Agricultural Extension, working with livestock farm advisors:

1 pound of lettuce	23 gallons
1 pound of tomatoes	23 gallons
1 pound of potatoes	24 gallons
1 pound of wheat	25 gallons
1 pound of carrots	33 gallons
1 pound of apples	49 gallons
1 pound of chicken	815 gallons
1 pound of pork	1,630 gallons
1 pound of beef	5,214 gallons

- Number of calories of fossil fuel expended to produce 1 calorie of protein from soybeans: 2
- Number of calories of fossil fuel expended to produce 1 calorie of protein from corn or wheat: 3
- Number of calories of fossil fuel expended to produce 1 calorie of protein from beef: 54
- Amount of waste (stored in open cesspools) produced by North Carolina's 7 million factory-raised hogs compared to the amount produced by the state's 6.5 million people: 4 to 1
- Relative concentration of pathogens in hog waste compared to human sewage: 10 to 100 times greater

WORLD HUNGER

- Number of people whose food energy needs can be met by the food produced on 2.5 acres of land:

If the land is producing cabbage	23 people
If the land is producing potatoes	22 people
If the land is producing rice	19 people
If the land is producing corn	17 people
If the land is producing wheat	15 people
If the land is producing chicken	2 people
If the land is producing eggs	1 person
If the land is producing beef	1 person

- Amount of grain needed to adequately feed every person on the entire planet who dies of hunger and hunger-caused disease annually: 12 million tons
- Percentage by which Americans would have to reduce their beef consumption to save 12 million tons of grain: 10

CONSUMERISM: FACTS AND STATISTICS

These statistics are excerpted from *All Consuming Passion: Waking up from the American Dream* (3rd edition, 1998), a pamphlet produced by the New Road Map Foundation and Northwest Environment Watch. All statistics are cited and sourced in this pamphlet, which is available for $1 from the Simple Living Network (800-318-5725).

TIME, TV, SHOPPING, AND ADVERTISING

- American parents spent 40% less time with their children in 1985 than they did in 1965
- Percentage of free time spent watching TV: 40
- Amount of time the average American will spend watching TV commercials: almost 2 years of his or her life
- Amount of time the average American spends either watching TV or behind the wheel of a car: the equivalent of one day out of every week
- Number of high schools in the U.S. in 1996: 24,000
- Number of shopping centers in the U.S. in 1996: 42,130
- Average time per week spent shopping in 1985: 6 hours
- Average time per week spent playing with children in 1985: 40 minutes
- Number of new toys issued each year by American toymakers: 3,000 - 6,000

- Spending on toy advertising:
    1983: $357 million
    1993: $878 million
- Americans spend twice as much on children's athletic shoes than they do on children's books

MONEY, SPENDING AND QUALITY OF LIFE

- Percentage rise in per capita income in the U.S. since 1970: 62
- Percentage decrease in quality of life in the U.S. since 1970, as measured by the Index of Social Health: 51
- Percentage of disposable personal income in the U.S. allotted to savings:
    1980: 8.2
    1995: 4.5
    1997: 2.1

ANIMAL TESTING: A PARTIAL LIST OF COMPANIES THAT DO NOT TEST THEIR PRODUCTS ON ANIMALS

ABBA Products, Inc.
Abracadabra, Inc.
Aubrey Organics
Aura Cacia, Inc.
Auromere Ayurvedic Imports
Autumn Harp, Inc.
Avalon Organic Botanicals
Aveda
Avon Products, Inc.
Ayurveda Holistic Center
Axtec Secret
Banana Boat Products
Bath & Body Works
Beauty without Cruelty
Biogime Int'l, Inc.
The Body Shop
Brookside Soap Co.
Clear Vue Products, Inc.
Clearly Natural Products, Inc.
Clinique
Conair Corporation
Compassionate Consumer
Crabtree & Evelyn, Ltd.
Deodorant Stones of America
Desert Naturels

Dr. Broner's "All One" Products
Dr. Hauschka Cosmetics
Earth Science, Inc.
Ecco Bella
EcoSafe
Ecover Products
Eden Botanicals
Estée Lauder Cos.
Bon Ami Company
Frank T. Ross & Sons, Ltd.
Giogio
Green Ban
HERC Consumer Products
Home Service Products Co.
Jason Natural Cosmetics
Jean Naté
John Paul Mitchell Systems
Jojoba Resources, Inc.
Kiss My Face
KMS Research, Inc.
KSA Jojoba
Levlad, Inc.
Life Tree Products
Lotus Light Enterprises

Louice Bianco Skin Care, Inc.
Marcal Paper Mills, Inc.
Mary Kay Cosmetics
Naturade
Natural Bodycare
Naturally Yours, Alex
Nature's Gate
Nature's Plus
Nexxus Products Company
Nirvanan, Inc.
Norelco
Oasis Brand Products
Orange-Mate, Inc.
Orjene Cosmetic Co., Inc.
Oxyfresh Worldwide, Inc.
Pamela Marsen, Inc.
Paul Penders
Peelu Products, Inc.
PetGuard
Pents 'N People, Inc.
Rachel Perry, Inc.
Rainforest Essentials
Redken Laboratories, Inc.
Reviva Labs, Inc.
Revlon, Inc.
Santa Fe Fragrance, Inc.

Sappo Hill Soapworks
SerVaas Labs, Inc.
Seventh Generation
Shaklee U.S., Inc.
Shikai Products
Sierra Dawn
Simplers Botanical Co.
Sinclair & Valentine
Sleepy Hollow
Sonoma Soap Company
St. Ives Labs, Inc.
Sumeru Garden Herbals
Sunshine Natural Products
Terra Nova
Tisserand Aromatherapy
Tom's of Maine
Trader Joe's Company
Ultima II
Unpetroleum
Vegelatum
Vermont Soapworks
Weleda, Inc.
Wella Corporation
WiseWays Herbals
Wysong Corp.
Yves Rocher, Inc.

In addition, look on individual products for the Corporate Standard
of Compassion for Animals logo (For more infor-

mation, contact: Julia Janak, Coalition for
Consumer Information on Cosmetics, P.O. Box
75307, Washington, DC 20013, 1-888-546-
CCIC.), which identifies companies that have
pledged they will neither conduct or commission
animals tests on finished products nor use any ingredient formulation
that is tested on animals.

SWEATSHOP-FREE LABOR AND FAIR-TRADE PRODUCTS

Coop America's website (<www.coopamerica.org>) maintains an up-to-date list of those companies which do and those which do *not* employ sweatshop labor. They also publish their national Green Pages (<www.greenpages.org>): it lists companies which adhere to fair trade and environmental standards as well as companies which sell organic and environmentally friendly foods, products, and clothing. Please visit these websites for information on specific companies and products. Coop America has also created the following checklist that consumers can use when they visit retail stores.

COOP AMERICA'S CHECKLIST FOR PRODUCTS MADE WITHOUT SWEATSHOP LABOR

Ask the companies with which you do business the following questions:

- Does your company know how the workers who made this product were treated?
- Do you have a list of all the factories around the world that make your products?
- Does it include the wages and working conditions in each factory?
- Can I see the list?

- Does your company guarantee that the workers who made this product were paid a living wage, or enough to support their families?
- Are you providing development programs in the communities where your workers live?
- Does your company have a code of conduct that protects human rights and forbids child labor and unsafe conditions in all the factories that make its products?
- How do you enforce these rules?
- Are your factories monitored by independent, third-party sources?
- Are you working with others in your industry to come up with truthful, meaningful labels so consumers can know exploited labor wasn't involved in making your products?

GENETICALLY ENGINEERED FOODS

The nonprofit organization Greenpeace maintains an up-to-date website (<www.truefoodnow.org>) to inform consumers about which food companies do and which do *not* use genetically engineered ingredients. To find out whether the foods you buy contain genetically modified organisms (GMOs), visit this website. Since labeling GE foods is not required by law, it is up to consumers to find out whether or not their foods contain GMOs. You can use the suggested questions below as a guide when contacting companies.

To find out company policies and ingredients, call companies using their toll-free phone numbers, usually printed on the food packaging. Ask the company the following three questions (from the <www.truefoodnow.org> website):

1. Does your company support the consumers' right to know if foods are made with genetically engineered ingredients or ingredients derived from genetically engineered crops?
2. Does your company currently inform consumers by labeling whether you use genetically engineered ingredients or ingredients derived from genetically engineered crops in your products?
3. Does your company intend to eliminate genetically engineered ingredients and ingredients derived from genetically engineered crops from its products?

RESOURCES

RECOMMENDED BOOKS

Humane Education

Brookfield, Stephen D., *Developing Critical Thinkers*, Jossey-Bass, 1987.

Chaffee, John, *The Thinkers Way*, Little Brown, 1998.

Cornell, Joseph, *Sharing Nature with Children*, Dawn Publications, 1979.

Garbarino, James, *Raising Children in a Socially Toxic Environment*, Jossey-Bass, 1995.

Gatto, John Taylor, *Dumbing Us Down*, New Society Publishers, 1992.

Hammond, Merryl and Rob Collins, *One World, One Earth: Educating Children for Social Responsibility*, New Society Publishers, 1993.

Herman, Marina, Joseph Passineau, Ann Schimpf, and Paul Treuer, *Teaching Kids to Love the Earth*, Pfeifer-Hamilton, 1991.

Lickona, Thomas, *Educating for Character: How our Schools can Teach Respect and Responsibility*, Bantam, 1991.

Luvmour, Sambhava and Josette, *Everyone Wins! Cooperative Games and Activities*, New Society Publishers, 1990.

Miller, Alice, *For Your Own Good: Hidden Cruelty in Childhood and the Roots of Violence*, Trans. Hildegarde and Hunter Hannum, Farrar, Strauss, Giroux, 1983.

Miller, Ron, *Caring for New Life*, Foundation for Educational Renewal, 2000.

Palmer, Parker, *The Courage to Teach*, Jossey-Bass, 1998.

Seed, John, Joanna Macy, Pat Fleming, and Arne Naess, *Thinking Like a Mountain: Toward a Council of All Beings*, New Society Publishers, 1988.

Selby, David, *EarthKind: A Teachers Handbook on Humane Education*, Trentham Books, 1995.

Sheehan, Kathryn and Mary Waidner, *EarthChild: Games, Stories, Activities, Experiments and Ideas About Living Lightly on Planet Earth*, Council Oaks Books,1994.

Van Matre, Steve, *Earth Education: A New Beginning*, Institute for Earth Education, 1990.

Weil, Zoe, *Animals in Society: Facts and Perspectives on our Treatment of Animals*, Animalearn, 1990 (available from IIHE).

Weil, Zoe, *So, You Love Animals: An Action-Packed, Fun-Filled Book to Help Kids Help Animals*, Animalearn, 1994 (available from IIHE).

MEDIA AND GLOBALIZATION

Bagdikian, Ben, *The Media Monopoly*, Beacon Press, 1995.

Best, Joel, *Damned Lies and Statistics*, University of California Press, 2001.

Consumers Union Education Services, *Captive Kids: Commercial Pressures on Kids at School*, Consumers Union Education Services, 1995.

GAO Report, *Public Education: Commercial Activities in Schools*, U.S. General Accounting Office, 2000.

Jacobson, Michael F. and Laurie Ann Mazur, *Marketing Madness*, Westview Press, 1995.

Kilbourne, Jean, *Can't Buy My Love*, Simon and Schuster, 1999.

Klein, Naomi, *No Logo*, Picador, 1999.

Korten, David, *When Corporations Rule the World*, Kumarian Press, 1995.

Lasn, Kalle, *Culture Jam*, William Morrow, 1999.

Mander, Jerry, *Four Arguments for the Elimination of Television*, William Morrow, 1978.

McChesney, Robert W., *Rich Media, Poor Democracy*, University of Illinois Press, 1999.

McKibben, Bill, *The Age of Missing Information*, Plume, 1993.

Molnar, Alex, *Giving Kids the Business: The Commercialization of America's Schools*, Westview Press, 1996.

Quart, Alissa, *Branded: The Buying and Selling of Teenagers*, Perseus, 2003.

Quinn, Bill, *How WalMart is Destroying America*, Ten Speed Press, 1998.

Quinn, Daniel, *Ishmael*, Bantam/Turner, 1992.

Postman, Neil, *Amusing Ourselves to Death*, Penguin, 1985.

Stauber, John and Sheldon Rampton, *Toxic Sludge is Good for You*, Common Courage Press, 1995.

Steyer, James P., *The Other Parent: The Inside Story of the Media's Effect on Children*, Atria Books, 2002.

Summers, Sue Lockwood, *Media Alert! 200 Activities to Create Media-Savvy Kids*, Hi Willow Research and Publishing, 1997.

Welton, Neva and Linda Wolf, *Global Uprising: Confronting the Tyrannies of the 21st Century*, New Society Publishers, 2001.

Winn, Marie, *The Plug-In Drug*, Penguin Books, 1985.

HUMAN RIGHTS

Bales, Kevin, *Disposable People*, University of California Press, 2000.

Ehrenreich, Barbara and Arlie Russell Hochschild, *Global Woman: Nannies, Maids, and Sex Workers in the New Economy*, Metropolitan Books, 2002.

Faludi, Susan, *Backlash: The Undeclared War Against American Women*, Anchor Books, 1991.

Jensen, Derrick, *The Culture of Make Believe*, Context Books, 2002.

Johnson, Allan G., *Privilege, Power and Difference*, McGraw Hill, 1997.

Kielburger, Craig, *Free the Children*, HarperPerennial, 1998.

Kressel Neil J., *Mass Hate: The Global Rise of Genocide and Terror*, Westview Press, 2002.

Szwarc, Josef, *Faces of Racism*, Amnesty International, 2001.

SOCIAL CHANGE

Abdullah, Sharif, *Creating a World that Works for All*, BK Publishers, 1999.

AtKisson, Alan, *Believing Cassandra: An Optimist Looks at a Pessimist's World*, Chelsea Green, 1999.

Callander, Meryn G. and John W. Travis, *A Change of Heart*, Arcus Publishing, 1993.

Elgin, Duane, *Voluntary Simplicity*, William Morrow, 1993.

Fuller, Robert W., *Somebodies and Nobodies: Overcoming the Abuse of Rankism*, New Society Publishers, 2003.

Hammond, Allen, *Which World?: Scenarios for the 21st Century*, Island Press, 1998.

Hartmann, Thom, *The Last Hours of Ancient Sunlight*, Mythical Books, 1998.

Jones, Ellis, Ross Haenfler and Brett Johnson, with Brian Klocke, *The Better World Handbook: From Good Intentions to Everyday Actions*, New Society Publishers, 2001.

Loeb, Paul Rogat, *Soul of a Citizen*, St. Martin's Press, 1999.

Moyer, Bill, *Doing Democracy: The MAP Model for Organizing Social Movements*, New Society Publishers, 2001.

Robbins, Ocean and Sol Solomon, *Choices for Your Future*, Book Publishing, 1994.

Shi, David, *The Simple Life*, Oxford University Press, 1985.

Seo, Danny, *Be the Difference: A Beginner's Guide to Changing the World*, New Society Publishers, 2001.

ENVIRONMENTAL ISSUES

Carson, Rachel, *Silent Spring*, Houghton Mifflin, 1962)

Ehrlich, Paul and Anne Ehrlich, *Betrayal of Science and Reason*, Island Press, 1996.

Goldbeck, Nikki and David, *Choose to Reuse*, Ceres Press, 1995.

Greer, Jed and Kenny Bruno, *Greenwash: The Reality Behind Corporate Environmentalism*, Third World Press, 1996.

Hawken, Paul, *The Ecology of Commerce*, HarperBusiness, 1993.

Meadows, Donella, Denis Meadows, and Jorgen Randers, *Beyond the Limits*, Chelsea Green, 1992.

Orr, David, *Earth in Mind*, Island Press, 1994.

Ryan, John C. and Alan Thein Durning, *Stuff: The Secret Lives of Everyday Things*, Northwest Environment Watch, 1997.

Shiva, Vandana, *Water Wars*, South End Press, 2002.

Tobias, Michael, *World War III*, Continuum, 1998.

State of the World books by the Worldwatch Institute, Washington, DC.

Wackernagel, Mathis and William Rees, *Our Ecological Footprint*, New Society Publishers, 1996.

ANIMAL ISSUES

Cavialleri, Roberto and Peter Singer, *The Great Ape Project*, St. Martins Press, 1993.

Donovan, Josephine and Carol Adams, eds., *Beyond Animal Rights*,: Continuum, 1996.

Eisnetz, Gail, *Slaughterhouse*, Prometheus, 1997.

Mason, Jim, *An Unnatural Order*, Continuum, 1997.

Masson, Jeffrey Moussaieff, with Susan McCarthy, *When Elephants Weep*, Delacorte, 1995.

Newkirk, Ingrid, *Free the Animals*, Noble Press, 1992.

Scully, Matthew, *Dominion*, St. Martin's Press, 2002.

Singer, Peter, *Animal Liberation*, Avon, 1975,1990.

Spiegel, Marjorie, *The Dreaded Comparison*, Mirror Books, 1996.

HEALTH AND DIET

Barnard, Neal, *The Power of Your Plate*, Book Publishing, 1990.

Lappé, Frances Moore, *Diet for a Small Planet*, 20th anniversary ed., Ballantine Books, 1991.

Lappé, Marc and Bailey, Britt, *Against the Grain: Biotechnology and the Corporate Takeover of Your Food*, Common Courage Press, 1998.

Lyman, Howard, with Glen Merzer, *Mad Cowboy*, Scribner, 1998.

Marcus, Erik, *Vegan: The New Ethics of Eating*, McBooks, 1998.

McDougal, John, *The McDougal Program for a Healthy Heart*, Dutton, 1996.

Ornish, Dean, *Dr. Dean Ornish's Program for Reversing Heart Disease*, Ivy Books, 1996.

Robbins, John, *The Food Revolution*, Conari Press, 2002.

Schlosser, Eric, *Fast Food Nation*, Houghton Mifflin, 2001.

Shiva, Vandana, *Stolen Harvest: The Hijacking of the Global Food Supply*, South End Press, 2000.

COOKBOOKS

Barnard, Tanya and Sarah Kramer, *How it All Vegan*, Arsenal Pulp Press, 2000.

McCarthy, Meredith, *Sweet and Natural*, St. Martins Press, 1999.

Pickarski, Brother Ron, *Friendly Foods*, Ten Speed Press, 1991.

Raymond, Jennifer, *The Peaceful Palate*, Heart and Soul Publications, 1992.

Sass, Lorna, *Complete Vegetarian Kitchen*, Hearst Books, 1992.

Stepaniak, Joanne and Kathy Hecker, *Ecological Cooking*, Book Publishing, 1991.

Stepaniak, Joanne, *The Uncheese Cookbook*, Book Publishing, 1994.

Tucker, Eric and Westerdahl, John, *The Millennium Cookbook*, Ten Speed Press, 1998.

Wagner, Lindsay and Spade, Ariane, *The High Road to Health*, Fireside, 1990.

RECOMMENDED PERIODICALS

The Atlantic Monthly

Green Teacher

E Magazine

Earth Island Journal

Hope Magazine

Mothering Magazine

Mother Jones

Multinational Monitor

Orion

The Progressive

Utne

SATYA

Yes! A Journal of Positive Futures

VegNews

WorldWatch

Z Magazine

ORGANIZATIONS AND WEBSITES

The list of websites below includes nonprofit organizations that attempt to alleviate suffering, raise awareness, and prevent destruction. This list does not include industry sites or groups funded largely by industry. If you look at the list, my bias becomes clear: I want you to have information about protecting our planet, its people and its animals. This choice of websites is also meant to balance the perspectives that are promoted by well-funded industries and by the expensive curricula that these industries are providing free of charge to schools. I don't want to imply that these are the only sources of information on these topics; rather, they are meant to offer alternative views to industry opinions. For corporate perspectives you can usually go to the website listed on a specific product. There are also groups whose goal is to promote the use of certain resources or products (e.g. coal, nuclear energy, paper, biomedical research, etc.), and you can find these sites by simply doing a search on the subject, for example "coal" or "nuclear energy."

HUMANE EDUCATION

Association of Professional Humane Educators
    <www.aphe.humanelink.org>

Bridges of Respect <www.bridgesofrespect.org>

Center for Non-Violent Communication <www.cnvc.org>

Circle of Compassion <www.circleofcompassion.net>

Humane Education Advocates Reaching Teachers (HEART)
    <www.nyheart.org>

The Empathy Project <www.empathyproject.org>

The E.T.H.I.C. <www.The-ethic.org>

International Institute for Global Education <www.oise.utoronot.ca>

International Institute for Humane Education <www.IIHEd.org>

National Association for Humane and Environmental Education
    <www.nahee.org>

New World Vision <www.newworldvision.org>

Roots and Shoots <www.janegoodall.org/rs>

Seeds for Change Humane Education
    <www.seedsforchangehumaneeducation.org>

Yes! Tour <www.yesworld.org>

MEDIA/CULTURE

Adbusters Media Foundation <www.adbusters.org>

Center for Media Education <www.cme.org>

Center for New American Dream <www.newdream.org>

Commercial Alert <www.commercialalert.org>

Fairness and Accuracy in Reporting (FAIR) <www.fair.org>

National Institute on Media and the Family
  <www.mediaandthefamily.org>

Simple Living Network <www.simpleliving.net>

Simply Enough <www.simplyenough.com>

Stop Commercial Exploitation of Children
  <www.commercialexploitation.com>

TV Turnoff Network <www.tvturnoff.org>

HUMAN RIGHTS AND SOCIAL JUSTICE

Amnesty International <www.amnesty.org>

Anti-Slavery International <www.antislavery.org>

Coop America <www.coopamerica.org>

Fair Trade <www.fairtrade.org>

Free the Children <www.freethechildren.org>

Human Rights Watch <www.hrw.org>

The Hunger Project <www.thp.org>

Infact <www.infact.org>

Southern Poverty Law Center <www.splcenter.org>

United Students against Sweatshop <www.usasnet.org>

ENVIRONMENT

Circle of Life Foundation <www.circleoflifefoundation.org>

Earthsave <www.earthsave.org>

Earth Island Institute <www.earthisland.org>

Friends of the Earth <www.foe.org>

Greenpeace <www.greenpeace.org>

Native Forest Council <www.forestcouncil.org>

Rainforest Action Network <www.ran.org>

Rainforest Foundation <www.savetherest.org>

Student Environmental Action Coalition   <www.seac.org>
Worldwatch Institute <www.worldwatch.org>

ANIMAL PROTECTION

Animal Protection Institute <www.api4animals.org>
Doris Day Animal League <www.ddal.org>
Endangered Species Coalition <www.stopextinction.org>
Farm Sanctuary <www.farmsanctuary.org>
Farm Animal Reform Movement (FARM) <www.farmusa.org>
Fund for Animals <www.fund.org>
Humane Farming Association <www.hfa.org>
Humane Society of the United States   <www.hsus.org>
International Fund for Animal Welfare <www.ifaw.org>
People for the Ethical Treatment of Animals
     <www.peta-online.org>
Tribe of Heart <www.tribeofheart.org>
United Poultry Concerns <www.upc-online.org>

FOOD AND DIET

Safe Tables Our Priority (STOP) <www.stop-usa.org>
Food First <www.foodfirst.org>
Center for Food Safety <www.centerforfoodsafety.org>
Organic Consumers Association <www.purefood.org>
Pesticide Action Network <www.panna.org>
North American Vegetarian Society <www.navs-online.org>
Greenpeace's True Food shopping list <www.truefoodnow.org>
VegSource Interactive <www.VegSource.com>

SCIENTISTS AND DOCTORS FOR REFORM

Center for Science in the Public Interest <www.cspinet.org>
Physicians Committee for Responsible Medicine <www.pcrm.org>
Physicians for Social Responsibility <www.psr.org>

Canadian Assoc. of Physicians for the Environment
 <www.children.cape.ca>

Union of Concerned Scientists <www.ucsusa.org>

POLITICAL REFORM

Accurate Democracy <www.accuratedemocracy.com>

America Speaks <www.americaspeaks.org>

Campaign Finance Reform <www.publicagenda.org>

MoveOn.org <www.moveon.org>

Public Citizen <www.citizen.org>

INDEX

ACKNOWLEDGMENTS

Writing these acknowledgments is a daunting task. It is simply impossible to thank all of the people who have contributed to this book. I am indebted to the many activists around the world who have brought to public awareness the plight of people and animals and the dangers to the ecosystem, and to the writers, scholars, journalists, and researchers who have devoted their lives to gathering and disseminating information so that we might learn from their efforts. It is thanks to them that we are able to make informed choices and create a more humane world.

Mary Ann Naples worked with me on this project every step of the way, not only as my agent but also as a superb editor and advisor. Her counsel was always right on target, and her enthusiasm for and commitment to this book have meant more to me than I can possibly say. I feel very privileged to be represented by her.

It is an honor to have my book published by New Society Publishers, a company dedicated to improving the world by publishing books that promote sustainable living, justice, and compassion. I was personally committed to having *Above All, Be Kind* printed on recycled paper with nontoxic ink and discovered, to my delight, that NSP prints all of its books on 100% post-consumer, recycled paper and uses only vegetable-based inks. It's a pleasure to work with a publishing company that truly walks its talk. I am very grateful for all the suggestions, support, and ideas from everyone I've worked with at NSP, especially publisher Chris Plant and copy editor Michael Mundhenk.

To the people I interviewed for this book — thank you for your wise words and wonderful stories! David Berman, Dani Dennenberg, Craig Kielburger, Carrie Lang, Ocean Robbins, Danny Seo, and Khalif Williams are each an inspiration to me, as I hope they are to you. To their parents who raised them to be such humane and exceptional people, you have my utmost admiration and appreciation. In particular, a special thank you to John Robbins (Ocean's dad) and Ellen Berman (David's mom), with whom I conferred while writing this book. I am also grateful to Kathy Kandziolka and Erika Straus-Bowers for the stories they shared with me about their childhood.

To my readers — Jayne Arata, Edwin Barkdoll, Mary Pat Champeau, Caryn Ginsberg, Mark Lesser, Nancy Mellon, Dawn Ray, Caroline Sulzer, and Khalif Williams — thank you for your honest critiques and excellent suggestions. This book is much, much improved because of you.

My husband and I are very lucky to be raising Forest in a community of extraordinary people and parents. These pages are filled with their wisdom, insights, ideas, and parenting skills, both verbally shared and observed. A few deserve special mention: Mary Pat Champeau, Francoise Gervais, Patty Herklotz, Mary Ellin Logue, Buzz Masters, Moira McMahon, Nancy

Plouffe, and Dawn Ray, to whom I have turned for parenting (and other) advice on more occasions than I can count, often during our own gatherings of mothers — thank you! And to the women of the Gift circle — the safety you provide makes all things possible and endurable. Special thanks to Catherine and Scott Springer, whose parenting advice I solicit regularly and whom I admire immensely, and to Rebekah Raye Woisard, my role model for kindness.

To the faculty and administrators at The Bay School — thank you for creating an environment that fosters not only learning but also citizenship, kindness, and community. Thank you, too, for your unswerving commitment to all your students, our children, and for your openness to us parents.

There are many people who are working to make humane education an integral part of each child's education. Their work is what will make it that much easier for parents to raise their children to be humane because parents' efforts will be reinforced in schools. I am deeply grateful to our board of directors at The International Institute for Humane Education (IIHE) and to the students in our M.Ed. and certificate programs. To Rae Sikora — I offer my sincere thanks for all I learned from and with you during the years we worked together. To current and former Komie Grant recipients Dani Dennenberg, Melissa Feldman, James LaVeck and Jenny Stein, Andie Locke, Sarah Spaulding, and Freeman Wicklund — thank you for being pioneers and devoting your lives to creating a humane world through humane education. To Brad Goldberg and the Animal Welfare Trust and Marjo and Jim Kannry — thank you for making so much of this work possible through your support. And to Steve Komie, who has done more to advance humane education than perhaps anyone through his extraordinary commitment and generosity — what can I say? The humane education movement will be successful largely because of you.

IIHE has a small but amazing staff, and I am so grateful for our wonderful team. Manager/Development Director Khalif

Williams' commitment to humane education, to his work at IIHE, and to becoming the best person he can be is awe-inspiring. Thank you for all you do, Khalif. You will be an extraordinary father.

Mary Pat Champeau, coordinator of our M.Ed. degree and certificate programs, has been my primary sounding board for this book since the first germ of the idea several years ago. I feel not only blessed by our friendship, but also by her humor and wisdom. When I call her the Buddha, it's only partly in jest.

Bob St. Peter was our part-time administrative assistant while I was writing this book, and he taught me through example each day he was in the office. He embodies a beautiful combination of quiet perseverance and unswerving commitment to justice.

Caryn Ginsberg is an IIHE board member, but it's hard to remember that she's not on staff because she consults with us almost daily (on a volunteer basis). I can't imagine where IIHE would be without her remarkable intellect, perceptiveness, and utter calm.

My friend Jayne Arata lays bare the truth with so much love that I am safe to explore just about anything with her. When I was too nervous to show the early drafts of chapters to anyone, I showed them to Jayne, who promptly gave me her excellent editorial advice without mincing words. There are simply no words to describe the depth of my gratitude.

Many thanks to my mother, Peggy Weil, for her constant support and commitment to my work and for modeling volunteerism throughout my childhood, and to my father, the late Stanley Weil Jr., whose enormous, undemanding, and unconditional love has been the most sustaining gift of my life. Thanks also to my brother, Stanley Weil III, who gave me valuable advice when I first embarked on this project.

My husband Edwin Barkdoll is not only my most thorough and painstaking editor, has not only taught me more critical thinking skills than anyone else, and is not only my beloved partner in life, he is also a wonderful father to Forest, which may be the greatest blessing of all.

A final few words for Forest: I hope that writing this book has helped me be a better mom to you, and that it will help to create a more humane world for you to grow up in. If ever I'm failing to raise you humanely, feel free to remind me to read my own words!

Zoe Weil
Surry, Maine, 2003

ABOUT THE INTERNATIONAL INSTITUTE FOR HUMANE EDUCATION

The International Institute for Humane Education (IIHE) is dedicated to creating a world where kindness, respect, and compassion are the guiding principles in our relationships with all people, animals, and the Earth. IIHE works to achieve this goal by training individuals to be humane educators and by advancing comprehensive humane education worldwide.

In 1997, IIHE established the first Humane Education Certificate Program (HECP) in the United States, and, in 2000, through an affiliation with Cambridge College, began offering a distance-learning Master of Education degree in Humane Education, also a first in the U.S. IIHE leads weekend humane education workshops in the United States and abroad, and each year trains hundreds of people to be humane educators who, in turn, reach thousands of students.

Headquartered in Surry, Maine, IIHE's beautiful facility is situated on 28 oceanfront acres overlooking the mountains of Acadia National Park. The grounds include an organic garden, a woods trail, and a pebble beach where seals, eagles, loons, and osprey are frequently seen. To learn more, please visit our website at <www.IIHEd.org> or email us at info@IIHEd.org.

ABOUT THE AUTHOR

Zoe Weil is president of The International Institute for Humane Education (IIHE) and the author of several humane education books for young people. A humane educator since 1985, Zoe now trains others to be humane educators through IIHE's graduate and certificate programs in humane education. She and her husband, Edwin Barkdoll, live in coastal Maine with their son, Forest. You can visit IIHE's website at <www.IIHEd.org> or contact Zoe at zoe@IIHEd.org.

If you have enjoyed *Above All Be Kind*,
you might also enjoy other

BOOKS TO BUILD A NEW SOCIETY

Our books provide positive solutions for people who want to
make a difference. We specialize in:

Sustainable Living ✦ Ecological Design and Planning
Natural Building & Appropriate Technology ✦ New Forestry
Environment and Justice ✦ Conscientious Commerce
Progressive Leadership ✦ Resistance and Community ✦ Nonviolence
Educational and Parenting Resources

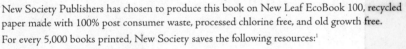

New Society Publishers

ENVIRONMENTAL BENEFITS STATEMENT

New Society Publishers has chosen to produce this book on New Leaf EcoBook 100, recycled
paper made with 100% post consumer waste, processed chlorine free, and old growth free.
For every 5,000 books printed, New Society saves the following resources:[1]

39	Trees
3,533	Pounds of Solid Waste
3,887	Gallons of Water
5,070	Kilowatt Hours of Electricity
6,422	Pounds of Greenhouse Gases
28	Pounds of HAPs, VOCs, and AOX Combined
10	Cubic Yards of Landfill Space

[1]Environmental benefits are calculated based on research done by the Environmental Defense Fund and
other members of the Paper Task Force who study the environmental impacts of the paper industry.
For more information on this environmental benefits statement, or to inquire about environmentally
friendly papers, please contact New Leaf Paper – info@newleafpaper.com Tel: 888 • 989 • 5323.

For a full list of NSP's titles, please call **1-800-567-6772** *or check out our web site at:*

www.newsociety.com

NEW SOCIETY PUBLISHERS